Under the Cover of Chaos

Under the Cover of Chaos

Trump and the Battle for the American Right

Lawrence Grossberg

PLUTO PRESS

First published 2018 by Pluto Press
345 Archway Road, London N6 5AA

www.plutobooks.com

Copyright © Lawrence Grossberg 2018

The right of Lawrence Grossberg to be identified as the author of this work
has been asserted by him in accordance with the Copyright, Designs and
Patents Act 1988.

British Library Cataloguing in Publication Data
A catalogue record for this book is available from the British Library

ISBN   978 0 7453 3792 0   Hardback
ISBN   978 0 7453 3791 3   Paperback
ISBN   978 1 7868 0269 9   PDF eBook
ISBN   978 1 7868 0271 2   Kindle eBook
ISBN   978 1 7868 0270 5   EPUB eBook

This book is printed on paper suitable for recycling and made from fully
managed and sustained forest sources. Logging, pulping and manufacturing
processes are expected to conform to the environmental standards of the
country of origin.

Typeset by Stanford DTP Services, Northampton, England

Simultaneously printed in the United Kingdom and United States of America

For Stuart Hall and Doreen Massey

Contents

Preface   viii

PART I   FROM TRUMP TO THE CONJUNCTURE

1   The Terror and the Beast   3
2   Telling Stories and Stories Told   16
3   Other Stories are Possible, and Possibly Even Better   31

PART II   IN SEARCH OF THE CONJUNCTURE

4   The New Right   53
5   The Reactionary Right   68
6   Affective Landscapes   91

PART III   A CONJUNCTURAL POLITICS

7   Back to the Present: A Reactionary Counter-modernity   113
8   Conclusions?   143

Appendix: Cultural Studies and Conjunctural Analysis   155
Bibliography   159
Thanks   165

Preface

These are dark times and getting darker every day. It never lets up. Significant time has passed since Trump's presidential victory and many people are still in disbelief, asking how did this happen? What does it mean? His presidency has not calmed things down; rather, it has augmented people's uncertainty and anxiety. And this is true not only in the United States. I know that many people around the world are concerned, in deeply visceral ways, about Trump; in each place, the political content and emotional valences of that concern are shaped by their own social context, the distributions of hope and possibility, and the forms of closure and constraint. Still, I want to talk about the U.S., which has once again become, quite literally perhaps, the belly of the beast. There is a real crisis. After all, the political culture and practice of governance is already a disaster, apparently rising to new levels of incompetence, deception, dishonesty, cruelty and greed, a deeply inhumane practice of governance. The combination of a bombastic, egotistical president, Republican control of Congress, and a conservative majority Supreme Court promises devastating consequences for democracy, global stability and peace, environmental recovery, sane economic policies, political freedoms, healthcare, cultural diversity, social justice and the social safety nets that are increasingly necessary.

In the U.S., many who oppose Trump and the Republican agenda are panicked; some of them run around like Chicken Little, screaming it's the end of the world.[1] Others try to find a way to

---

1. It is, of course, not just Trump. It is Trump and climate change, nuclear weapons, population growth, social hatred, etc.—and these problems presumably exist without Trump. But it is also Brexit, the decline of

shut out the increasingly absurd realities, but you can't escape it, no matter how hard you try. Politics has once again become the lingua franca of everyday life, and has come to define the mood of the country. Psychologists and pundits offer advice about how to cope with it, and the complex emotions it is soliciting. There is a sense of suspense—as everyone (whatever political position they may occupy) waits for the next shoe to drop. But the suspense is always accompanied by other emotions: fear and anxiety, certainly, but also anger and shock, and often, no small amount of laughter, all wrapped up in a bundle of panic. Even so, there are inevitably different responses, with different valences, to the present situation. But none of these, even from those who choose active resistance, seem able to create an aura or even much of a glimmer of hope.

For some, there is a kind of political despair. We are on the road to fascism or at least totalitarianism, and we are offered all sorts of "warnings from history." We "argue" about whether it is *1984*, or *Brave New World*, or *A Handmaid's Tale*. (I prefer *Robocop* or perhaps the city of Qarth in *Game of Thrones*.) Or perhaps we have finally reached the final stage of the capitalist victory over democracy and social welfare—the apotheosis of greed.

For others, the situation is even worse, undercutting the very possibility of political reflection and reaction. We are amazed by how "low" Trump's campaign was willing to go to win.[2] Trump's election (and even his nomination) may even be evidence that the nation is no longer capable of self-government. And the continuing allegiance of his supporters simply exacerbates and legitimates one's sense of hopelessness. There are many allusions

democracy, the increasingly dangerous tone of foreign relations, and even the U.N. talks about the "worst humanitarian crisis" since its founding.

2. In the 1993 movie, *The Pelican Brief*, Supreme Court Justice Rosenberg says, "It never ceases to amaze me what a man will do to get into the Oval Office."

to the difficulty of keeping one's sanity, of maintaining one's equilibrium. Nothing seems to make sense. The world seems to be falling into chaos.[3]

There has also been an exhilarating explosion of vital and diverse forms of organizing and expressing resistance, even if it all feels rather drained of hope: so many marches, protests, petitions, efforts to defeat one piece of legislation or another, endless emails and fundraising requests, and millions upon millions of dollars spent on local elections turned into national referendums on Trump. A proliferation of organizations, media and campaigns— so many that it is hard to know what they are and to remember which ones one supports.

And yet, paradoxically, at the same time, people continue to live their "normal" lives, carrying on their business "as usual" to varying degrees, albeit increasingly living out an intensification of partisan sentiments. One might hope that we could find a more measured response to this contradiction between panic and normalcy and more effective forms of both opposition and popular exhortation.

What binds these responses together is their fixation on the figure of Trump and his presidency, which appears to be a singular—and singularly frightening—event. After all, he is a paranoid, narcissist, racist, misogynist, xenophobe, nationalist, isolationist, nepotist, anti-globalist, pro-global corporatist, ignorant, dissembling, and incompetent billionaire (?) claiming to speak for "real" Americans. He constructs the media/press not only as *his* enemy, but as the enemy of the nation, thereby justifying his own efforts to silence and exclude media coverage, but also his not-so-subtle endorsement of violence against

---

3. Keeping up with the list of inanities, contradictions, lies, inappropriate behaviors, etc. has become an obsession; the problem is, over time, it is easy to begin to normalize it, and take it for granted. See, e.g., David Leonhardt and Stuart A. Thompson, "Trump's Lies," *New York Times*, June 23, 2017. https://www.nytimes.com/interactive/2017/06/23/opinion/trumps-lies.html?_r=0

journalists. He constantly draws a picture of American carnage, of American decline, even of America as a dark and dangerous place, with little connection to reality. And then he offers empty promises of making America great again, without ever telling us how that is to be measured or accomplished. He is a demagogue, a con artist, the worst sort of emotional predator. He does not appear to understand or care about the Constitution or how government works.

All of this is true, but it does not necessarily tell us how to respond, or how to make sense of what's going on. In fact, this fixation and the panic organized around it may be part of the problem, as it becomes, oxymoronically, a normal, everyday obsession and an ordinary taken-for-granted reality. I have seen many friends (as well as the media) compulsively keeping meticulous records of his lies and absurd claims. I have heard compassionate and intelligent critics demonizing Trump (and the Republicans) with the same kind of absolute negation and hatred that the Tea Parties normalized in their vision of Obama as the devil and liberals as anti-white authoritarians. Such actions out of panic, resulting in demonization and a rush to visions of the enemy as beyond comprehension, redemption or compromise, are, I believe, not the best starting point, however understandable. Panic begets more panic and in the end, it is dysfunctional. I have no doubt that there are similarities between Trump's administration and forms of fascism and totalitarianism, but I do not think they are sufficient yet to warrant the conclusion that Trump is a fascist, or that we are becoming fascist, for many of the practices identified are common to many forms of demagoguery, authoritarianism and populism. Besides, I have heard this too many times before: many leftists were certain that G.W. Bush was a fascist as well. In fact, I will argue, much of what Trump is doing simply continues—albeit also inflates—practices that have become the norm of U.S. politics during the past forty or more years. No doubt Trump is and will continue to be a terrible president.

While, at the time of writing, he seems incapable of even forcing the Republican Congressional majority to bend to his will and his demands (e.g., Obamacare, tax cuts, relations with Russia), he continues to operate, often under the radar, to attack all sorts of regulations and regulatory agencies, to defund education and science, and to disrupt the already dangerously small stabilities of international relations. But the U.S. has had more than a few truly bad presidents. And no doubt, we should be afraid of the damage he will do (even beyond the damage already done by various New Right regimes), but we should also remember that we were right to be afraid after the electoral victories of Reagan and Bush, to take only the most recent examples.

On the other hand, wonderful and important as the many acts and organizations of resistance, opposition and alternatives may be, the impact of these important energies has been questionable, and they have been largely unable to transform despair and anger into hope, or opposition into unity. It is disheartening, I must admit, seeing the liberal/left embroiled in many of the same internal debates about tactics that have defined its fragmentation for fifty years: class vs. "identity," movement vs. party, horizontal vs. vertical, local vs. national, symbolic vs. disruptive vs. pragmatic, etc. It is even more disheartening that there is so little real discussion around possible disagreements about tactical effectiveness, or long-term strategizing. Too often, the opposition to Trump is simply appropriating and proliferating tactics that, one might think, have proven to be ineffective over the past decades—and certainly more recently. I do not deny the value of collective action, and the importance of constructing a sense of community, collective empowerment and moral reassurance. But surely that is the beginning and not the end of political engagement.

Political commentator Molly Ivins famously said, "Vote, write, work, march, sue, organize, fight, struggle—whatever it takes to secure the blessings of liberty." I have no doubt that many people, including Trump supporters, would agree wholeheartedly.

That may be a symptom of the fact that we are in something of a transitional moment, in which the old is dying and the new cannot yet be born. But what Ivins did not include (and what I think some elements on the right have also understood or at least used to understand) is the vital need to think, study, investigate, analyze, understand. Every political campaign involves four kinds of problems: messaging, visioning, strategizing and "theorizing" (or if you prefer, diagnosing or critically analyzing what's going on). Each of these is involved in the effort to tell different and better stories, but the progressive opposition often seems completely focused on the first two and not very concerned with the latter.[4] In the present moment, resistance is not enough! Even offering alternative visions will not do it. If progressives are to change the vectors of historical change, we will need strategies that get the nation from where it is to where we want it to be, and that means knowing a great deal more than we do about where the country—and the various constituencies across various dimensions—actually is.

---

4. Chris Lundberg has pointed out to me that political messaging involves principle and policy. Increasingly, conservative Republicans foreground principles, often to the exclusion of policy details. Liberal Democrats increasingly start with policy, only arriving at principle as a defense of policy. But there is a second dimension: Republicans tend to state principles or goals in the simplest, most absolute forms (e.g., destroy Islamic terrorism), while Democrats tend to present the nuances or complexities of their principles (e.g., destroy Islamic terrorism but let's remember that not all Muslims … and that we have contributed to the context … and there are consequences to our actions …). It is not that the latter are mistaken, but rather, that one must think about where and how complexity belongs, especially in rhetorical contexts. Messaging that foregrounds strong, simple principles lends itself to the sorts of affective politics that I will describe here. It is interesting to note that this difference—between emphasizing principle or policy, also characterizes in part the split between the Democratic Party and the movement left.

The story I offer here comes from a sense of urgency and fear, but also a refusal of the paranoia and panic—and the rush to understanding—so common among the progressive opposition, as well as a refusal to make it all about Trump himself; it is a response to the shadow of even darker times yet to come. Thus, I want to slow down the ways we think and talk about what's going on, because only if we think about *how* we think about the contemporary political context, can we avoid simply reasserting what we assume we already know, and relocating ourselves within an emotional or affective landscape of anxiety, panic and hatred, which may in fact be a significant part of the political culture we want to challenge.

I want to tell one possible story here—perhaps the most nightmarish story I can imagine out of the present circum-stances. And my urgency comes from my disappointment that the complicated, agonistic conversations one might have expected about "what's going on," have not really taken shape. So much has been written about what's going on—and much of it is filled with insights, although much of it is banal and predictable—but there are few compelling stories and even fewer real efforts to collabora-tively advance our collective understanding. It is disheartening to see that many people, including academics and journalists, seem all too ready to assume that they know not only how Trump's electoral victory happened but what exactly is happening, i.e., what it means for the future. Rather than conversation, we have a cacophony of voices, too often defined by assumed positions and practices, and increasingly subjected to moral surveillance.

What I offer here is not some starkly original interpretation, but an assembling of observations and ideas from all sorts of places that I have discovered along the way, to tell what I hope is a compelling and frightening story. I am not trying to provide the evidence that might persuade people that my story is right; my all-too-infrequent examples, data and anecdotes are meant to invite readers to provide their own supporting or dissenting realities. My hope is to begin constructing some common ground for the sort of diagnostic work and real political conversation that are the preconditions for figuring a way out of these dark times. We may fail, and such work may not be sufficient, but it is necessary. It will not bother me (well, maybe just a little) if my effort to assemble a different story fails. Failure is always an option; the question is, can one use it productively?

PART I

From Trump to the Conjuncture

I

The Terror and the Beast

The most obvious and pervasive feature of Trump's highly visible and almost entertaining (think of Alec Baldwin on *Saturday Night Live*, a guilty pleasure if ever there was one) if also terrifying performance, is the normalization of a frenetic chaos and hyper-activism. His erratic control of the executive state apparatus, his constant policy shifts and contradictory statements, his various appointments and firings, have everyone not merely baffled but always uncertain as to what is going on. The sheer unpredict-ability of what he will do next, of how he will respond to any challenge or even question, heightens the fear and incompre-hension. People seem to assume that this is a further sign of his dementia or incompetence, for surely, this cannot be his intention. And while I do not want to suggest that the chaos is his intention, we should take it more seriously, and think about whether there may not be some intentionality behind it, some reason for it. If nothing else, it seems to provide a context in which Republicans can blithely abandon many of the basic principles of conservatism in favor of a scorched-earth policy aimed at dismantling 150 years of social modernization.

The chaos also seems to have permeated the responses of those opposed to Trump as well, creating its own kind of frenetic hyperactivism, so that, e.g., proliferating numbers of marches are randomly announced (often online) with little time for organization, planning and preparation, or for evaluation and strategizing. People find themselves battered from one side to the other, so that the specific response we have one day seem inappropriate the next (e.g., the left's relation to FBI director Comey). And it has permeated as well our efforts to understand what is going on. A chaos of power, opposition and intelligence! My hypothesis is, if you will, that the chaos is the productive and strategic ground for at least some of the political trajectories and projects at work today.[1]

Of course, there are various possible and even credible interpretations of Trump's electoral victory, and the subsequent political and cultural developments that are taking the country, and less directly, many parts of the world, into an uncertain future. There are any number of different stories that could be constructed, and any number of still ill-defined futures that might be actualized, depending on subsequent actions and struggles. I want to offer one story, without any guarantees that it is necessarily the "right" one, or even the most likely outcome of current events; but it is perhaps the most frightening one (short of global destruction) and therefore worth considering.

If we are to understand what is happening, we should resist the all-too-common temptation to start by assimilating the specific to the general, making Trump into the U.S. version of something that is happening in many parts of the world: the emergence of nationalist (anti-global) and populist (anti-elitist and anti-establishment) formations, often expressed as discourses of racism (anti-immigration[2]) and forms of authoritarianism.

---

1. Recently, the historian of economics Philip Mirowski, in his book *Never Let a Good Crisis Go to Waste* (London: Verso, 2013), has argued that the contemporary experience of chaos, ignorance and doubt is a strategy of the Mont Pelerin Society (which included Friedrich Hayek and Milton Friedman amongst its members), a key source of neoliberal ideas of free-market capitalism and political libertarianism. Without disagreeing, such conspiracy theories ignore the complexities of history and context, and assume that intent guarantees success.

2. It is worth pointing out that, despite the headlines, the U.S. does not have an immigration crisis! We do not have "floods" of immigrants

(They have won in some places—Turkey and India, and appear to be on the rise in many other places, including parts of Europe and South America). These are often described as formations of demagoguery, authoritarian populism, neo-fascism, or illiberal democracy.[3] But these developments, especially anti-elitist and nationalist populism, can find other political expressions: for example, they have also been attached to more democratic and progressive agendas (e.g., in Spain, Greece and previously, in South America, but also in the U.S., in Sanders's presidential campaign). And they have fueled an even more radical, anti-establishment politics, dedicated to exiting, undermining or even "blowing up" the whole system, as in Italy's Five Star movement and elements of Spain's Podemos. While there are obvious relations amongst these different formations, I think it is more productive to start by examining the specificity of the contemporary U.S. context, in this case, of Trump's electoral victory and subsequent administration.

This effort might also lead us to reflect on the relation or difference between populist and popular politics, as described by Stuart Hall. A populist politics is built upon a construction of a frontier or line of demarcation and difference between "the people," which as a result is often a taken-for-granted and generally homogeneous entity, and the ruling bloc, which can be differently constructed but is almost always cast as "the elite."

---

pouring into the country, or waiting to pour in even if illegally. Perhaps, some have argued, the problem is not quantitative but qualitative, i.e., it is a problem of current immigrants' refusal to assimilate. This too is ill-informed, for the history of immigration in the U.S. suggests not only that it takes several generations for immigrants to adopt and adapt, but also that the processes of "becoming American" have never been purely assimilative, for immigrants do not give up their difference and the "American" culture does not remain unchanged as it adapts to immigrants.
3. Illiberal democracy generally refers to a nationalist politics defined by the rule of a majority without minority rights, and a rejection of political pluralism.

Populist politics is a politics of them versus us. Populist politics, in its rejection of the existing elite, can often fall back into purely affective or emotional appeals, making it susceptible to anti-intellectualism or to at least a marked decline in intellectual self-reflection.[4] A popular politics, on the other hand, sees "the people" as the ever-changing result of struggles to create a unity-in-difference, defined neither by its opposition to an other, or by a single, shared politics. A popular politics engages people "where they are" to forge a common set of struggles.[5]

To look ahead for a moment, I want to take the chaos of the contemporary context seriously, to argue that it embodies a particular sort of crisis, a particular moment of transition, a turning point rather than a tipping point. And while I will argue that this moment has to be understood historically, it does feel like something new is happening. It does feel like the terms of struggle, of knowledge, history and feeling, are changing, that there is a shift in the "tectonic plates" that have defined modernity. The question that needs to be asked is not so much about Trump but about the complex forces that have constructed him and the possibilities that they have brought into the mainstream political culture of the U.S.

I will suggest, first, that for the most part, the issues that define contemporary political struggle (and to a large extent, Trump's victory) have not significantly changed over the past decades, although the weight given to them and the ways they are rhetorically present have changed. I will contextualize the present moment by locating it in the continuing history of and struggle

---

4. However much one dislikes the "New Right," it started out with brilliant intellectuals like William Buckley and, I am sorry to say, it has deteriorated ever since. I wonder if those on the right would say something similar about progressive intellectual work (e.g., from C. Wright Mills and Herbert Marcuse to Noam Chomsky and Naomi Klein)?

5. See Stuart Hall, *The Hard Road to Renewal: Thatcherism and the Crisis of the Left* (London: Verso, 1988).

over, post-war conservatism, starting with the "New Right," a shifting set of alliances among various conservative and neo-conservative fractions and pro-capitalist (neoliberal, globalizing) forces who have struggled for over fifty years to win control of the Republican Party and now have apparently succeeded in winning control of the federal state apparatuses, as well as the majority of more local state governments. Much of what is most frightening about Trump's politics (both his strategies and at least some of his policies) is really the continuation and culmination of highly strategic struggles by which the "New Right" has, to a large extent, been able to prevent disagreements, however serious, from overshadowing the need to continually construct forms of unity, cooperation and even compromise that will enable it to realize its vision of another modernity, one that is significantly different from what the "New Right" takes to be the dominant "American liberalism" established in the post-war years. The results of this continuing effort will no doubt be devastating and frightening, and we must do all we can to mitigate the harm and ensure that it is short-lived.

But, ironically, just when the "New Right" seems to have succeeded, its control of the party has become problematic. Its sense of unity and control was fractured in recent years by the insurgency of the Tea Parties and the increasing visibility and power of the reactionary right. Over the years, there has been a broad range of "movement conservatives," with varying distances from and relations to a Republican Party increasingly defined by the "New Right." There have always been reactionary fringe groups, which occupied a position like the closeted relative whom one brings out on occasion; their very presence put pressure on others to accept as "normal" what might otherwise be seen as a form of abnormality or extremism.[6] While groups such as the

---

6. We might compare this to the way the apocalyptic "Christian identity movement" was talked about during the administration of G.W.

paleo-conservatives—represented at times by Barry Goldwater and Pat Buchanan—achieved some national visibility, they were always treated as something of an embarrassment, always pushed to the outer reaches of acceptability by an increasingly conservative Republican Party. Other groups—white supremacists, militia, and neo-Nazis, for example—were excluded and denied any legitimacy or visibility, and yet, they continued to exist at the outer limits of movement conservatism. These reactionary conservatives— it is not quite clear in what sense they are conservatives—are extremely fractured[7] and unwilling to compromise, but they share a broad hatred of modern forms of social and political life and organization, and modern commitments to critique, change and an openness to the new and unfamiliar. They are not merely anti-liberal modernists (the "New Right"), but anti-modernists or even pre-modernists. Perhaps they can be described as celebrating parochialism and tribalism (a kind of imagined pre-modern national-cultural fundamentalism) against cosmopolitanism and progress.[8] And so, what we have on the right itself is a struggle over modernity itself, increasingly understood as globalism and

---

Bush. Many people thought that its adherents provided deep direction and unacknowledged motivation, but they were never allowed to sit at the public table.

7. I will later identify five major forms of reactionary politics that have become part of public political discourses: white supremacists, Tea Party populists, right-wing counter-culturalists, neo-reactionary intellectuals and what I will call "Trumpist" intellectuals. Some of these groups describe themselves as "alt-right," a term that makes them sound too innocuous, like an underground rock band. The idea of the alt-right is even contested among the various groups, and ill-defined in the popular political imaginary.

8. For a wonderful re-reading of parochialism, see Meaghan Morris, "On the future of parochialism: globalization, *Young and Dangerous IV* and Cinema Studies in Tuen Mun," in J. Hill and K. Rockett (eds.). *Film History and National Cinema: Studies in Irish Film 2* (Dublin: Four Courts Press, 2005), pp. 17–36.

multiculturalism, a struggle over what it means to be modern, and the attempt to wrest its definition out of the hands of those who are seen to have been in control for almost a century.

Trump's campaign and electoral victory has allowed these reactionary groups to enter the stage of mainstream politics and even, to some extent, has legitimated them enough so that they can enter the ruling bloc. Their position might be described now as at the popular fringe at the center of the right. It will not matter that Trump may eventually fire Steve Bannon—one of the key point men for some of the reactionary right in the Trump administration—and other figures of the various populist and anti-populist reactionary right, from the White House; he has brought them (and their cultural and communicative practices) onto the stage of popular and political culture. We have a war within the right! And even more frightening, the reactionaries seem to be winning, pulling many from the "New Right" into more reactionary statements and positions. This contradiction in the right is both responsible for, and possible because of, the chaos, as an unintended attempt to hold in tension two very different projects and formations of conservatism, to say nothing of different visions of capitalism and different forms of racism. It is this chaos that speaks simultaneously of "America" as catastrophe and as "great."

Thus, the story I want to tell is not about Trump. I do not think that what's going on is all about Trump, that he is the main protagonist, or the driving force. Nor is he a malleable figurehead being manipulated by some master puppeteer (capitalism?). Nor is he simply an entertainer meant to distract us from the real story. Rather, assume that he is, like so many of us, caught by forces not entirely understood or controlled, but he has learned to "ride" or perform them as it were. For at least a moment, he is necessary, but neither sufficient nor guaranteed. But to what? And why is he seemingly indispensable? To a more complicated story about the right than is often told,[9] a story of a coming battle between two imaginations of the Right, of which Trump is the (accidental?) host? Is Trump the figure through which these contradictions could be played out in the fields of common sense and popular calculation? "Trump" holds together the opposing and often contradictory elements that are being articulated into a new political conservatism, embodying a variety of forms of nationalism, racism and capitalism. The sense of chaos that permeates his practices of governance is crucial, as is the ambiguity of his position as businessman, entrepreneur and entertainer who refuses even as president to give up these roles. The very complexity of his position enables him to live the chaos in the relations between family, nation and business on the one hand, and the relation of government and global corporate capitalism on the other, figuring himself as a crystallization of the crisis and the figure of a solution to the empire of chaos.

How Trump does this work takes me to the second argument I want to make, the second way I want to describe the current context, for it is accomplished in affective rather than ideological terms. What is affect? It is an essential dimension or ingredient of the messiness of human experience, and it is at least as complicated as the other dimensions—of biological bodies, social relations and structures, and meaning and consciousness (the latter having pre-occupied western philosophy at least since the Enlightenment).[10] Like the plane of meaning, affect is the contingent

---

9.   I have tried to begin such a complicated story of the contemporary left in my previous book, *We All Want to Change the World*. https://www. lwbooks.co.uk/sites/default/files/free-book/we_all_want_to_change_ the_world.pdf

10.   There are many definitions and theories of affect, including, at one end of the spectrum, theories of the ontological differentiation of bodies according to their capacities to affect or be affected, or of affect as purely material or bodily intensities, or psychoanalytically inflected models of energetics flowing in and across bodies, to, at the other extreme, affect

product of human and non-human events, contradictions and struggles. It varies over time and place, and is unevenly distributed across populations. If meaning is how we make "sense" of what is going on, affect is the energy that permeates all our experiences and defines what it feels like to live in a moment. Like meaning, affect is always constituted in the space between individuality and sociality, between consciousness and materiality, between the knowable and the not-yet-articulated. Affect encompasses a variety of ways in which we "feel" the world in our experience, including moods, emotions, maps of what matters and of what one cares about, pleasures and desires, passions, sentiments, etc.

The current political context has been constructed by appropriating and articulating certain practices and discourses from/into an emergent, affective landscape (comprised of several structures of feeling—the socially defined organizations in which we experience our lives[11]) that I will call "passive nihilism." Affect—the lived texture of experience—is the medium and agency by which the old is rearranged and made new, even as the new is slotted into long-standing relations. Like the common-sense maps of meaning in which we find the sense of our experiences, affective landscapes are the effects, both directly and indirectly, of many events and struggles, although they are never completely within our control, never completely the expression of a singular conspiracy or victory.

---

as socially determined, individually experienced emotions. My own use of the term sees it in terms of social feelings, moods, sentiments, etc. It is a complex but essential dimension of the "messiness" and multidimensionality of lived social reality that is the embodied effect of a variety of forms of discursive or semiotic formations. Therefore, for the most part, it is not communicated through some unmediated transmission, touch, or contagion. It is characterized by, but not reducible to matters of intensity.
11. See Raymond Williams, *The Long Revolution* (London: Chatto and Windus, 1961), and *Marxism and Literature* (Oxford: Oxford University Press, 1978).

Trump seems to offer himself up as an uncompromising, partisan wrecking ball (to quote a different "working-class" voice) that has been sent in to blow up the establishment, defined by the occupation of political and cultural institutions by a liberal/left alliance of elitists and multiculturalists, which has produced "American carnage." They are to blame for the fact that the state has (we might all agree) failed to solve the many problems facing our society. Hence, Trump's very style is the message, which may explain why some of his supporters took his campaign promises literally, while others made fun of his critics precisely because the critics took his promises literally. The most quotidian social practices, and the most normalized political practices—the definitions of civility, respectfulness, propriety and reasonable-ness—are inseparable from the struggles between different groups for power, status and resources. Trump's self-absorption, his lies, his personal attacks, his boastfulness, his vulgarity, his inappro-priateness, his corruption, even his bodily presence—are the performance of his refusal of business as usual. But such practices of civility are precisely what represses the violent contradictions of our sociality. The fact that such norms, which define acceptable forms of social relations, are inoperative, may contribute to the increasing visibility and violence of racism, misogyny, etc. While Trump is not the first figure on the right to behave in ways that challenge the behavioral norms in which power hides itself—remember Pat Buchanan, Ann Coulter and Sarah Palin, all of whom are representatives of reactionary conservatism—he does not seem to allow anything to restrain or constrain his behavior. His performance of incivility is a political statement, a tactical and "white-washed" inversion of other (working-class and urban black street culture) performances of incivility. It is ironic that the left apparently does not remember that it has often been accused of acting inappropriately, in ways that were not "nice" and that it has, at times, championed such forms of "carnivalesque" behavior as a political tactic.

I want, then, to tell a better story about what's going on amidst the chaos. The notion of a better story is crucial to my efforts, although it is a metaphor at best. I could also talk about a better map or assemblage.[12] They all figure the process of reconstructing or re-articulating a context. Still, it is perhaps easier to ask, what makes a better story? I think there are three conditions: First, it embraces the complexity and contradictions of what is happening, since this is precisely what constitutes the specificity of the context we struggle within and against. A better story refuses to reduce that context to some simple explanation (it's really all about …); it refuses to simply apply or conclude with generalities (e.g., yet another populist nationalism). Second, it seeks to find the openings, the possibilities for change, for redirecting events in a different direction. Leonard Cohen, in one of my favorite songs, writes "There is a crack in everything. That's how the light gets in." A better story searches for the cracks that might make some previously unseen paths visible.

And third, it seeks to speak to people where they are (not where we think they should be, not where we already have judged them to be), and to speak to them in the languages and logics that they understand, to move them, at whatever pace is possible, along those newly uncovered paths. A better story is strategic, reflecting on where, when and how complexity is embodied and used. A better story does not try to tell people what they *should* feel but to grasp and change what they *do* feel. Does the left actually know what people feel today? Does it know what they want? What they

---

12. This image of intellectual work comes from my own commitment to cultural studies, especially as it is embodied in the work of Stuart Hall, as a way of doing rigorous political-intellectual work. See Stuart Hall, *Cultural Studies 1983* (Durham, NC: Duke University Press, 2017). And while my own formation is at the border between British and U.S. cultural studies, the project has been taken up and given shape in many regions of the world. See my *Cultural Studies in the Future Tense* (Durham, NC: Duke University Press, 2010).

believe in and might be willing to fight for?[13] Does it understand their rage, fears, uncertainties, anxieties, hopes, desires? Even more, does it know what possible ethical ground might justify its claiming to know what people should feel?

I hope that my story will do at least two things: first, it will provide a richer if still partial context for understanding what's going on, and second, it will tell a truly frightening story of one possible outcome of the forces defining that context: the emergence of what I will call "reactionary counter-modernity." There is no guarantee that this will be actualized or, if it is, in what precise form. But if, in the short term, we should be afraid, in the long term, perhaps we should be even more afraid. The real question I want to pose, then, is how are the various fractions of the left going to prepare for and respond to this struggle within the right? And the warning I wish to offer is that, whether we like it or not, the opposition to Trump and to the various conservative strategies are also shaped by this history of the right, and operate on the same affective landscapes. It is commonly said that one cannot escape one's worldview (or ideology) but it is even more difficult—for both the right and the left—to act outside existing affective landscapes. At the very least, this should lead us to search for new kinds of reflective strategizing and new kinds of countervisions that speak to people's desires, and wrestle with their sense of possibilities.

In the next two chapters, I will contrast two ways of telling the story about what's going on. The first, which describes a struggle between two camps, sets the terms for most accounts of Trump's victory. The second offers a different—conjunctural—story, built on the demand to contextualize and thereby, embrace

---

13. For the most part, the left has rarely come to terms with the deeply held beliefs and skepticisms of large parts of the population, or how we might make sense of them and, more importantly, how can we organize a politics that takes this seriously?

the complexity of current events and states of affairs. Chapters 4 and 5 present the histories of U.S. post-war conservatisms briefly discussed above. Chapter 6 describes the emergent affective landscape of "passive nihilism" that, I believe, is profoundly determining the shape of current actions and relations. I will identify four structures of feeling that comprise this landscape: affective autonomy (hyperinflation, fundamentalism and fanaticism), anxiety, temporal alienation, and narcissism. Chapter 7 brings the results of these investigations together to offer a description of three of the most powerful tendencies of the emergent formation of reactionary modernity: the primacy of culture (and affect), the complex transformations of forms of cultural mediation, and a new political imaginary (of a nation without a state and a popular, alt-fascist corporatocracy). Chapter 8 brings it all back home: pessimism of the intellect, optimism of the will. Being a baby-boomer, I cannot avoid comparing the present moment to the 1960s. In the 1960s, we "knew" that profound changes were afoot but we did not have an adequate sense of what they were, so our efforts to get ahead of those changes and have some control over the directions of history had, at best limited success. Today, we find ourselves caught in a moment of potentially even more momentous change and we need to find ways to get ahead of it. We need to find more grounded and effective ways to shape the future rather than just always reacting defensively, after the fact. And we need to find new sources and forms of optimism, new visions that open the possibility of getting from here to somewhere better. Change is inevitable, but its direction and content are never guaranteed.

2

Telling Stories and Stories Told

Let me describe my project and its assumptions. I believe that it is the responsibility of political intellectuals to tell the best story they can. There are many kinds of stories that can and should be told, including those aspirational stories that attempt to define where we would like to be. Such stories are built upon assumptions about human nature, the nature of reality, and the inter-relationships that define the possibilities of various modes of being in the world. These are generally, especially when told from a progressive position, optimistic stories, filled with hope and, usually, visions of peace and love, although they are increasingly juxtaposed with apocalyptic narratives about the path we are on. But I don't want to tell another aspirational story here.[1] There are also political-strategic stories of how we get from where we are to where we want to be, and diagnostic stories that tell us where we are. I believe that such diagnoses are a necessary beginning if we are to understand the challenges we face and to develop adequate strategies to fight against the forces and alliances that are pushing the U.S. (and indirectly, the world) in certain directions, for how can you know where and how to fight if you do not know what you are fighting against? And how can you know where you can

---

1. Many of the current aspirational stories are similar to if not identical with those that were being told in the 1960s; the difference seems to be primarily on the other side: the frequency and severity of the apocalyptic narratives that precede them.

get to if you do not know where you are? Bad stories make bad politics!

At their best, diagnostic stories are critical in the sense of looking beyond experience to its conditions of possibility, of searching for what enables us to experience what we do, to make sense of things the way we do, to think and know what we do, to feel how we do. They refuse to accept that politics simply reflects such experiences, feelings, etc., rather than articulating and refracting them. Philosophers and social scientists have long debated the nature of such conditions; some assume such conditions are universal, others see them as defining the actuality of the present and enabling us to imagine—and make—it otherwise. And for still others, they define the processes that have made our immediate and evident experience what it is (including the fact of its obvious naturalness); for this last position, critique demonstrates that what is presented as the beginning of a story is actually the end of a story yet to be told.[2]

A good diagnostic story does not assume that it already understands what is going on, nor does it seek to claim unearned optimism. Instead, it seeks out pessimism, attempting to discover and acknowledge just how bad things really are. Often, such efforts will reveal that conditions are even worse than one had assumed (or at least, that the real sources of despair may not be where one had been looking). It is only when one has arrived, through rigorous intellectual work, at the nadir of pessimism that one can begin to earn the optimism of the will that is itself the condition of possibility of struggling to transform the world.

---

2. These positions can be represented, respectively, by Kant, Foucault and Marx. The obvious example of the last is Marx's argument that classical political economy took the empirical given-ness of the market to be the reality of capitalism, while Marx found the condition of possibility of the capitalist market in the mode of production.

Generally, most diagnostic stories about political struggles in "dark times"—including most of the stories being told about Trump—see politics as a battle between two giant, relatively homogeneous camps standing opposed to each other across a single frontier: the left versus the right, progressives versus conservatives. In general, I do not think this kind of story is particularly useful, even if at first glance the world looks that way. If it does, it is most likely because one is standing with heart and mind firmly planted directly in the middle of one camp staring directly across at the other, eyes fixed on the most threatening, most extreme "regiments" of the enemy.

A common variation recognizes that the camps are not homogeneous but coalitions defined by ongoing efforts to bring the different groups into a consensus of overlapping values and visions. Such stories redefine unity in terms of a particular political calculus of popular support (electoral victories) and/or dissent (mass protests), while the groups themselves are usually equated with demographic or electoral constituencies. But such stories often falter when they have to deal with the contradictions between where people stand experientially, politically, ideologically and affectively; for example, despite the country's move over half a century toward the right, many if not most Americans continue to hold vaguely liberal positions on many of the most important policy issues. Furthermore, this kind of story cannot answer or is incapable of describing how a minority can hold power in such coalitions in supposedly democratic societies.

These are, to a large extent, the kinds of stories that are being told about Trump's electoral victory. They often begin with a series of reassuring if contradictory reminders. First, the very significance of the "victory" can be questioned. Clinton won the popular vote and only lost because of an institution designed to protect slavery and rural, under-populated states—although she got 5 million less votes than Obama did in 2012—so that Trump won with just over 17 percent of the population, gathering fewer votes than McCain in 2008 or Romney in 2012. And the Republicans have, for some time, been systematically working to reduce access to voting for likely Democratic constituencies. And besides, Clinton was an extremely unpopular candidate (beyond whatever misogynist impulses she may have released) and ran a disastrous campaign, leading significant numbers of voters to either stay home (over 45 percent) or vote for a third party candidate (6 percent generally, and 8 percent for 18–24-year-olds).

Second, we can always blame the media. After all, the media gave Trump billions of dollars of free exposure, of unmediated (!) coverage. How many times has the statement by the president of CBS been repeated? "It may not be good for America but it's damn good for CBS … The money's rolling in, and this is fun ….". The mainstream media waited too long before they started calling out Trump's lies, even while they were portraying Clinton in a particularly negative light. At the same time, the increasing polarization of the news media and the diminishing trust people have in the news (although presumably, everyone does trust their own source of news, just as many people who do not approve of Congress do approve of their own representative), created a crisis of truth. The problem is often laid at the feet of Fox News, which has dominated cable news for the last fifteen years and had more viewers than CNN and MSNBC combined during the election campaigns. Yet it claims (and is often treated by its viewers) not to be part of the "dominant" media, which is then positioned as the enemy.[3] But then, maybe the real problem lies with the Internet, where 62 percent of voters got their news. During the campaign, Facebook followed by Google were the primary sources of news and, as if to emphasize the problem, only a quarter of Americans used two or more websites. The fact is that the right has done

---

3. Remember that the Fox network was for many years cutting edge in terms of its entertainment programming, including, for example, *The Simpsons*.

a better job of occupying and "democratizing" social media and attracting popular audiences. Moreover, it has both unleashed and taken advantage of the emergence of fake news sites (usually characterized by a dizzying array of outrageous political headlines and a chaotic visual arrangement of attention-grabbing advertisements and merchandising offers) and the anti-communicative practice of trolling, which is often (but not always) driven in the first instance by economic greed and yet almost always ends up supporting the most extreme and reactionary conservative positions and candidates.

Third, the most immediate and widely accepted explanation of Trump's victory insists that the essence of Trump's support came from "*the* white working class," a population that has been ignored by the left and the establishment, and that increasingly feels (and perhaps is perceived by some) as superfluous, disposable, in decline. Such people supposedly feel that they have no future, or better, that they have been deprived of the future they were promised and deserve because they have worked diligently for it and have earned it. They are represented as living in places which don't matter to the rest of the country and the mainstream media; they are assumed to feel that they are unable to wield the machines of power to their own benefit. They feel that they have been wronged, wounded and abandoned by the government, by elites, and by others who have unfairly "cut in line" ahead of them. Those above them are getting rich, those below them are getting help in various forms. And those below them are the largely non-white beneficiaries of a "compensatory" politics that is, in essence, paying reparations to identity groups who claim to have been subjugated by the white (heterosexual) majority and as a result, have drawn all the attention, benefits and sympathies to themselves. As a result, members of the angry white working class feels that they are suffering without any compensation or assistance (for everything from health insurance to college tuition). They experience themselves as victims of people and forces outside of their own immediate lives and communities, in circumstances of economic and racial anxiety, which result in expressions of resentment, rage and even a reactionary desire for revenge. Further, apparently, these sentiments necessarily translate into a politics of anti-elitism and anti-liberalism (which may or may not be the same), racism, xenophobia and misogyny.[4]

For many, in the end, the election was all about the economy, about the anxieties provoked by job insecurity resulting from the loss of manufacturing (and other blue-collar) jobs, the debt crisis (and the resulting housing crisis that both brought about and was exacerbated by the "Great Recession" of 2008), and the declining economic, social and even geographical mobility that has made the American dream less palpable and less possible. This economic precarity apparently finds an outlet in the expression of racist insecurities, giving new life to an old argument—blaming Trump's victories on the new social movements, especially on various identity politics, as if they were merely distractions, which not only blinded both liberals and leftists to growing white working-class despair and anger, but also gave the white working class a strongly visible target to blame (as if these various identity groups could now be identified with cosmopolitan elites and government) and gave them a vocabulary (of identity victimage) they could appropriate. Identity politics has not only fragmented progressive forces but by taking away its primary focus on the economy, it has diluted its popular appeal.

It is perhaps necessary to say a word here about the notion of "identity politics," both to defend it and to clarify its failures. "Identity politics" is, simply put, too general a category to be particularly useful, for it covers over at least two sets of questions and contestation. The first asks whether identity is ever stable and fixed, whether any identity has an essential defining core, or

---

4. See Ghassan Hage, *White Nation: Fantasies of White Supremacy in a Multicultural Society* (London: Routledge, 2000).

whether every identity is always in process, a becoming rather than a being, defined only through relational practices and processes of differentiation.[5] The second demarcates the difference between fighting for an identity (a cultural matter) and fighting against various political practices that subordinate/oppress particular groups precisely by constructing the identities that are engaged. Race as identity is itself a result of racism, and since there are different practices of racism in different contexts, different ways of dividing and distributing people into categories of inclusion and exclusion, the very reality of "race" as an identity varies. Anti-racist politics is different than the defense of African American culture.[6] Thus, there are many racisms and many ways race is lived. And each legitimates, proscribes and even prescribes particular forms of actions and relations.

Blaming "identity politics" for the problems of the left is naïve at best. It is impossible to imagine a popular progressive strategy that would not put the full range of social and cultural injustices— issues of racism, sexism, homophobia, etc.—at its center, alongside questions of economic inequalities and political democracy. Any progressive politics must fight against practices that construct and subordinate such identities, and these cannot be reduced to matters of economics or redistributive justice. And it is also the case that matters of economics and resource distribution cannot

5.   Stuart Hall argued for such a contextual theory of race as difference, what Paul Gilroy calls anti-anti-essentialism. See, e.g., "New ethnicities," in Kobena Mercer (ed.), *Black Film, British Cinema, ICA Documents 7* (London: British Film Institute/Institute for Contemporary Arts, 1988), pp. 27–31; and "Who needs 'identity'?" in Stuart Hall and Paul du Gay (eds.), *Questions of Cultural Identity* (London: Sage, 1996), pp. 1–17. It is worth noting that intersectionality is largely an attempt to solve the problems of essentialism without actually abandoning it.
6.   See Paul Gilroy, *Against Race* (Cambridge, MA: Harvard University Press, 2002).

be addressed independently of these structures and practices of social differentiation and injustice.

Since identity politics is too general a category, one must only deal with specific forms of political and cultural activisms. Some current forms of "identity politics" have returned to essentialist understandings despite decades of political and theoretical criticism. And some continue to equate anti-racist politics with the defense of black culture, for example. More importantly, as I hope to make clear later, some contemporary practices seem to be expressions of the same conditions of possibility that are shaping emergent tendencies on the right. I am thinking here of the personalization of politics (we have moved from "the personal is political" to "the political is personal"), the appeal to experience and affect as the court of first and last appeal, the absolute politicization of truth, and the empowerment of victimage, which often result in forms of internal policing (aka political correctness, or PC). Without claiming that these practices are complicit with the right, they have too often provided discursive fuel for the right (and produced unnecessary fissures in the left).

There are in fact two versions of the story of the angry and abandoned white-working class. The first calls forth a sense of guilt and a rather uncritical sympathy for those who have been ignored. Putting aside any critical relation to ethnographic evidence, one tells stories romanticizing these populations as basically good people—the heart and soul of America, despite their racism, etc.—who embody the American virtues of hard work, family values, patriotism, etc., and now find themselves in unfair and incomprehensible circumstances not of their own making. One can hear in the background (and sometimes in the foreground) the echoes of Main Street and the virtues of small-town America!

But the opposite story is equally likely: we return to repeat—this time with the arrogance of righteous defeat—what we have been saying all along, telling stories that condemn Trump supporters. For example, we point out (yet again) that the reddest states (and even counties) are often the ones not only taking the most in government benefits and subsidies, but also giving back the least in taxes. That is, the states that pay the least taxes per capita get the most per capita benefits. And the states that pay the most taxes get screwed not only by the Electoral College but by the distribution of federal financial largesse. And then, in a startling reversal that goes largely unexplained, "those" people blame the government for the very failures for which they receive its help. The conclusion would almost necessarily be that these populations are "cultural dopes," at best suffering from false consciousness, acting against their own self-interests. Or alternatively, following a long tradition of policy discourses, the cultures of Trump supporters are described as self-reproducing pathologies, for example, cultures of poverty, in which their behaviors construct a spiral of declining well-being, continuing a long cosmopolitan tradition of negative judgments of these reactionary, retrograde, backwards, and anti-modern populations. These angry "white" voters are pictured as irrational, driven solely by despair and anger.[7]

Still, there are serious problems with what has quickly become the dominant narrative of Trump's victory: a narrative of white working-class resentment.[8] The first problem is that the "white working class" is never defined in any precise ways. It is never clear to whom these narratives refer: who is "the white working class"?

---

7. Other stories are beginning to emerge, largely from within the academy. One story triumphantly proclaims that big data will finally allow us to achieve the meta-view necessary for a science of social reality. Other stories claim that the present moment reveals the truth of theories that were written before their appropriate time as it were, revealing Trump as the simulacrum, the spectacle, the ultimate victory of the commodity, or of capitalism (yet again).

8. The discussion that follows is deeply indebted to the ongoing work of the COMM 750 "Class" Working Group, and their preliminary report: Ryan Brownlow, Jing Jiang and Megan Wood, "Disarticulating the white working class." A new version will be appearing: Megan Wood and Ryan Brownlow, "Not about white workers," *Lateral*, forthcoming.

It is sometimes an economic matter (blue-collar and agricultural workers?), sometimes a geographical matter (rural versus urban, Midwest versus the coasts), and sometimes a matter of education. The stories often conflate "the white working class" with rural and small-town populations and/or particular Rust Belt urban and suburban populations. The result is that a taken-for-granted notion of the (white, male) working class becomes the "figure" standing in for a more complicated and unstable sense of how class is discursively constructed out of the historically contingent conditions of social existence. The one thing we can be sure of is that the working class is never as simple, never as homogeneous, as these stories suggest.

Additionally, the story of the resentful working class makes three independent assumptions: that Trump won the white working class, that this support was vital to his victory (as it well may have been in a few key swing states), and that their support was the direct result of their economic decline and insecurity. Consider the last claim for a moment. After examining the evidence, Rothwell concludes:

> There appears to be no link whatsoever between greater exposure to trade competition or competition from immigrant workers and support for national security and economic policies in America, as embodied by the Trump campaign ... [It is] very unlikely that direct exposure to harm from globalization could be a causal factor in motivating large numbers of Trump supporters.[9]

In fact, he goes on to argue that those communities that were most directly affected by global competition were less likely to support Trump.

9. J. Rothman. "The lives of poor white people." *The New Yorker*, September 12, 2016. http://www.newyorker.com/culture/cultural-comment/the-lives-of-poor-white-people

The question then is who supported Trump and why. It is unclear that the "white working classes" were anything more than a fragment and not even the largest fraction of Trump supporters, nor is it obvious that Trump even won this ill-defined constituency.[10] If we control for race and age, those who voted for Trump were richer and at least as well educated as those who voted for Clinton. Clinton handily won non-white voters, regardless of income or education, while Trump won white voters, regardless of income or education. At first glance, it appears that Trump won the majority of voters with less than a college education, while Clinton won the majority of those with a college degree. And yet college-educated whites were over-represented while non-college educated voters were under-represented (according to the national percentages) among Trump supporters. While Clinton won a majority of women, Trump won a majority of white women (thus giving rise to the theory that it is all about race); he won more non-Christians and non-religious votes than any Republican since 2000.[11] While he outperformed Romney with Asians, Hispanics and young people, he actually did worse than Romney among whites and seniors. Trump even seems to have won over a significant number of people who voted for Obama and even some who approved of Obama's performance.

Finally, consider income, one of the most common indicators of class. The average median income of Trump supporters was $72,000, higher than that for both Clinton and Sanders, both of whom did significantly better with voters whose income was under $30,000. (Of course, one should note here that there is a general tendency for poorer people to be less likely to vote.) Trump had a slight advantage among supporters from households

---

10.   Nicholas Carnes and Noam Lupu, "It's time to bust the myth: Most Trump voters were not working class." *Washington Post*, June 5, 2017. http://tinyurl.com/y9dw6fvl

11.   Trump won the white evangelical vote by a large margin, making it one of the best predictors.

with incomes over $50,000, while Clinton had significantly higher support from households with income under $50,000. Trump apparently did a better job than Clinton of winning voters with household incomes between $50,00 and $199,000, who accounted for a majority of voters.

This does not describe a victory that depended on some imagined white working class, nor is it obvious that Trump captured most of this white working class. Trump's support clearly extended into significant numbers and fractions of the middle class and even a college-educated working class (a noticeable feature of the current job market). These fractions often own or manage businesses, or they occupy the sorts of skilled blue-collar jobs that have tradition-ally resulted in a "middle-class" lifestyle and social identity. Now it is probably true that many middle-class fractions are increasingly facing economic precarity and diminishing mobility. Maybe some share feelings of resentment, rage and anxiety. But neither of these statements is likely true of the majority of those who voted for Trump. Instead, it appears that for many Trump supporters, the anxieties and insecurities they experience are not about their own lives but about the lives of the next generations (their children and grandchildren) who are, it is assumed, unlikely to be able to reproduce the lifestyle of their parents and grandparents. In fact, the generation of 18–35-year-olds is, simultaneously, the most educated populations in U.S. history and largely, in both economic and occupational terms, likely to be significantly more working class. That is, the economic anxiety of these Trump supporters is a projection into the future and a judgment of the future present.

The second problem is that the dominant narratives of the resentful white working class assumes that the "ruling elites" (educated, cosmopolitan, multicultural, urban), including intellec-tuals, do not and have not listened to them, or even taken notice of them. Apparently, Democrats, leftists and intellectual elites have been living in a bubble, unaware of what is going on around them, refusing to hear the screams of despair and hopelessness coming from this population. The result has been the recent publication of and fascination with many actual ethnographies of this "ignored" white population.[12]

We would do better to recognize that such feelings of resentment, anti-elitism, anti-liberalism, racism and xenophobia, especially as these have been taken up and given populist expression, are not new among fractions of the white working, lower middle and even middle classes; they extend back at least to the America Firsters (and one might also include the various progressive parties of the early twentieth century), the Liberty League's opposition to the New Deal, and they were certainly visible in the 1960s (e.g., Barry Goldwater, attacks on New York's liberal mayor John Lindsay, etc.). Social critics have long written about the decline of small-town America and the image of an abandoned Main Street is one that constantly reappears, although the cause and the enemy changes (e.g., out-of-town malls). For C. Wright Mills and others, the rise of "the power elite," based on the increasing assumption that government was to be placed in the hands of an educated, technocratic bureaucracy (even if based on the assumption that this would mitigate forms of prejudice), posed real challenges to the possibilities of democracy.[13] As early as the 1980s, economists were describing the impact of "deindustrialization" and social commentators were talking about the links between economic and racial insecurity, about the resurgence of nationalism and anti-elitism, over the past decades. How could one not have seen them in the growing polarization and distemper of U.S. society over the

---

12. Among the most successful examples: Arlie Russell Hochschild, *Strangers in Their Own Land* (New York: The New Press, 2016); J.D. Vance, *Hillbilly Elegy* (New York: HarperCollins, 2016); K.J. Cramer. *The Politics of Resentment: Rural Consciousness in Wisconsin and the Rise of Scott Walker* (Chicago, IL: University of Chicago Press, 2016). Also Charles Murray, *Coming Apart* (New York: Crown, 2013).

13. For contemporary criticisms of meritocracy, see Chris Hayes, *Twilight of the Elites* (New York: Broadway Books, 2013) and Jo Littler, *Against Meritocracy* (London: Routledge, 2017).

past decades? None of this means that various governments and policies have not failed to successfully address these problems (or that some administrations gave various disadvantaged populations lower priorities) but it also does not mean that we can take for granted that the establishment technocrats were neither aware of nor concerned about working-class and rural populations.[14] But the sense that these problems have never registered on political and intellectual radar is a key part of contemporary populist narratives, and it is false!

The final problem is that the white working-class narratives do not get at some crucially important questions: Why—given the actuality of the rise of Republican power since the 1980s—do some people, many of whom have voted Republican for some time, feel they have had no political voice? How are such feelings—from rage to impotence—constructed, or better, how are they being reconstructed in the present context, and how are they being attached to specific political positions and hopes? And most importantly, why, at a certain moment, have a variety of people decided that their only option is to "send in the wrecking ball?" What choices have people made? What other options might they have taken? And why did they see this one as reasonable or desperate or both? What are the full range of sentiments that people invested in their choice?[15] How are various material conditions, sentiments and political positions being rendered equivalent? Without some

---

14. The fact is that while both Republican and Democratic policies may have clearly failed to satisfactorily ameliorate the deteriorating conditions, the federal government has spent significant funds in these areas.

15. I have argued before that, too often, we see choice and consent in binary terms: accept or reject, but they are more complicated events; they can be active or passive, dispassionate or passionate. They can be enthusiastic, limited, grudging, hopeful, desperate, disaffected, negotiated, ironic, recalcitrant, or forced, but choice can also be an expression of willful neglect, active avoidance, righteous indignation, enraged impotence, and so on, shading into multiple forms of rejection, resistance and escape.

consideration of these matters, without more complex analyses of the historical, material and social conditions of possibility, the forms of political and cultural labor that led to this outcome, and the variety of affective orientations that led to different forms and degrees of support for "the Trump option," I do not think that we can understand where we are and where we might be heading.

3

Other Stories are Possible, and Possibly Even Better

There is a different kind of diagnostic story—a conjunctural story, which begins by accepting that there is complexity everywhere and at every level. It recognizes that the fact that people think the problem is simple is simply part of the problem. It attempts to embrace and reconfigure the messiness of lived realities, to take account of the many and often contradictory "facts," experiences, statements, feelings, formations, projects, agents and determinations that define what is going on, rather than taking the more common route of simplifying or reducing reality to a simple story (often offered on the assumption either that this is all that "ordinary" people are capable of understanding or that the story-teller already knows what it is all about). It understands both history and power as the ongoing struggle to organize the complexities and multiplicities into structures that define moments of unity (identities) and relations of difference: white vs. people of color, rural vs. urban, parochial vs. cosmopolitan, educated vs. ignorant, self-conscious vs. duped, open-minded vs. close-minded, good people vs. racists, reasonable vs. fanatical people, reason vs. emotion, etc. Such identities and relations are not illusory; they are real but contingent. Reality is an organized multiplicity (chaos) but any particular organization is neither necessary nor guaranteed. Conjunctural stories are expressions of and responses to the lived realities, struggles and crises of people's lives. Consider for example Raymond Williams's reading of the long-standing opposition between "the country and the city" as different types of responses to, different manifestations or forms of expression of, a common but evolving crisis: "we must not limit ourselves to their contrast but go on to see their interrelations and through these, the real shape of the underlying crisis … the point … is not to disprove or devalue either kind of feeling. It is to see the real change that is being written about …."[1]

A conjunctural story does not see two camps across a frontier; it sees many groups, each with its own politics and concerns, moving closer to and further away from others, across temporal and spatial markers. It sees multiple sites of struggle around which different temporary coalitions are built, different values and visions struggled over, different battle lines drawn, and different weapons deployed (to carry the metaphor to its conclusion). Such a story is based on the recognition that people care about different issues, and have different logics and values which they use to think about the issues and evaluate the options. At each of these sites, some people will experience it as unstable, live it as a crisis; other groups may not, or may constitute the crisis differently. Any "crisis" then is a construct, which can find different expressions and responses; different groups will have different investments and they will have different modes of involvement and engagement, stretching from apathy to weak concern, to a willingness to compromise, to all-out war. Gramsci described this as a war of positions, an alternative to populist constructions of the people versus the elite.[2]

Sometimes, the multiple struggles and crises of social life come to increasingly define people's lives, and politicians, activists and intellectuals all attempt to make sense of them by assembling them into a larger single crisis—a complicated, fractured, unstable and

---

1. Raymond Williams, *The Country and the City* (New York: Oxford University Press, 1973), p. 297.
2. Antonio Gramsci, *Selections from the Prison Notebooks* (New York: International Publishers, 1971).

even contradictory but still unified national or, to use Gramsci's term, "organic" crisis. The crisis transforms society into a "problem space,"[3] which is neither objectively given nor merely subjectively experienced; it is constructed, the result of political struggle and competing narratives. At such a moment, the very identity and purpose of the nation is called into question. An organic crisis defines a vitally felt need for radical social and political change. It problematizes the defining values of a society, the common logics by which people's relation to and place in the world are understood and evaluated. Different constructions result in different maps of the war of positions; different stories of the organic crisis propose and enable different solutions or settlements; each tries to establish a unique balance in the field of forces by shifting the investments in, and the priorities and organizations of social relations and the distributions of resources. But all too often, such maps and stories are reduced to simple binary political choices, as though everything could be lined up into opposing camps. One can perhaps better understand the actual complexity of such a crisis by considering Stuart Hall's description of the failure of a new organic crisis to emerge in the Great Recession:

> The economy lies somewhere close to the centre of that issue. But, as Gramsci argued, though the economic can never be forgotten, conjunctural crises are never solely economic or economically determined "in the last instance". They arise when a number of forces and contradictions, which are at work in different key practices and sites in a social formation, come together or "con-join" in the same moment and political space and, as Althusser said, "fuse in a ruptural unity". Analysis here focuses on these crises and breaks. Do the condensation of forces, the distinctive character of the "historic settlements" and the

---

3. David Scott, *Conscripts of Modernity* (Durham, NC: Duke University Press, 2004).

social configurations which result, mark a new "conjuncture"? The present crisis looked at first like one which would expose the deep problems of the neo-liberal model. But so far it is a crisis which refuses to "fuse".[4]

At such moments, when a war of positions is lived as a set of crises that have not yet been successfully constructed as an organic crisis, many segments of the society are likely to experience the situation as an overwhelming state of chaos.[5]

A conjunctural story seeks to understand the specificity of what is going on by identifying as carefully as possible what is new and what is old, what is part of a longer history and what has been introduced into the current context, and then, how these multiple elements shape each other so that the old can take on new characteristics and effects, and the new can take up residual forms and resonances. A conjunctural story is built by a process of contextualization, locating any event (such as the election) in the context constructed by a complex set of relations and determinations. Any event exists as but one crystallization of, one way into, a broader and more complicated context.[6]

---

4. Stuart Hall, "The neoliberal revolution." *Cultural Studies* 25 (2011): 705.

5. If various political interests compete to construct the crisis in such a way that they appear to have the most likely solution, the most likely redefinition and redirection of the nation, and hence, deserve the power to lead the nation, even if people disagree with many of the particulars of their program, this is what Hall, in *The Hard Road to Renewal*, calls hegemonic struggle: it takes advantage and even organizes the war of position by entering into a series of negotiations and compromises with various constituencies in order to win their alliance at particular sites and their consent at a more general level. I do not think Trump's victory has been won through a hegemonic struggle, and the question of whether it constructs an organic crisis is open to analysis and debate.

6. Conjunctural analyses are at the heart of cultural studies, and I do believe that this is just the sort of moment for which it was designed.

I propose then to begin to offer a conjunctural story of what's going on, by giving an account of the contemporary context, and of how the emergence of Trump (and the possible emergence of a reactionary counter-modernity) is articulated by and rearticulates that context. My assumption is that such an account of the election or the configuration of forces that it has gathered together may give us a better foundation upon which to build oppositional strategies and imagine alternative and realizable futures. We might start with the things we do know about the context, even the most obvious.

We know that *the government seems incapable of meeting many of the challenges that we face* as a nation and as a world. And even though some would like to blame this on the Republicans (e.g., their obstructionism during the Obama presidency), did anyone think that Obama or Clinton was going to do what was necessary to sufficiently address the problems? In its most extreme expression, we might conclude that the governmental establishment—the systems, institutions and policies of post-war democracies—were designed to address problems that no longer exist (i.e., building a national economy, fostering international trade, shaping a national identity, creating systems of national public services) and is incapable of addressing the emergent problems and demands.

We know that *the demographics of the country are changing*, and the liberal/left has been screaming it from the mountaintops for decades. (The Republican Party was inevitably doomed! So what did we expect them to do? To die quietly and politely, or to do

---

Cultural studies emerged to deal with the complexities of a war of position and of struggles to construct an organic crisis, and one in which culture obviously played a crucial role, although it was not obvious what that role was or how culture was working. Cultural studies is made for moments where we don't know what's going on, and we don't yet know what theories, concepts and methods may enable us to find useful answers, or even to specify the questions. For a more academic note on conjunctural analysis in cultural studies, see the Appendix.

things, however unethical and even illegal we may think they are, to deny those emerging populations the ability to vote? Surprise!) And, we know that *socially legitimated forms of racism (such as criminalization and imprisonment) as well as the resegregation of housing and schools have become defining features of the country in the past decades.* Additionally, the U.S. has been the scene of increasingly visible and violent practices of hatred directed against people of color, women, immigrants, various ethnic groups, homosexuals, trans-people, etc. In many ways, this has often looked like a return to older, more legitimated (at the time) forms of condoned public violence and hatred,[7] even as the definitions and relations of race, gender, ethnicity, sexuality and culture are being reshaped.

We know that *we are in the midst of a major economic transformation.* If there is an economic crisis, it is of a different kind than the 1970s crisis of accumulation defined by the simultaneous existence of recession and inflation, or than that of the debt crisis of 2007–09. It is not only that GDP growth is declining in the advanced capitalist democracies. (In the U.S., it has gone from a yearly average of 2.3 percent between 1948 and 2000 to under 1 percent in the decade that followed and barely over 1 percent since then.) There has been as well (despite all the talk, even in universities) a declining rate of entrepreneurship—a declining number of start-ups, a declining number of self-owned businesses (down 65 percent since 1980 for those under 30), and a declining number of international patents.

We know that *this is connected to the changing distribution and nature of labor.* In 1900, about 38 percent of Americans workers were employed on farms, and about 31 percent in goods-producing industries (including extraction, construction and manufacturing). By the end of the century, those figures were under 3 percent and

---

7. One might think here of George Zimmerman's highly visible sale of the gun he used to kill Trayvon Martin in 2012, a symbolic act re-linking racial violence to capitalism and entrepreneurialism.

19 percent. In 1970, 25 percent of the workforce was in manufacturing; by 2005, it was under 10 percent. And the numbers continue to decline. Service industries (and what is now often called "affective labor") on the other hand increased from 31 percent to 78 percent. Of course, most of these changes are not unique to the U.S. Yet at the same time, this transition (which we do not yet perhaps understand) has created new and more jobs as the workforce has grown from 24 million (31 percent of the population) in 1900 to 142 million (44 percent of the population) in 2000. These changes are in large measure the result of the changing spatialization of economic relations (glibly described as globalization), the increasing possibilities of profits through financial transactions, and the increasing automation of all sorts of forms of physical and mental labor.[8] And these forces will continue to wreak havoc on older economic formations and those who cannot escape the limits they impose on our economic and social imaginaries.

We know that *we are emerging into a new kind of economy* but that the boundary between economic and social relations are blurring, not because everything is becoming a market (i.e., glib neoliberalism) but because of the emergence and infiltration of new technologies. I do not know what to call it because it has many expressions and forms, each of which has its own different history extending back in some cases to the 1950s and even earlier: information, digital, robotic, artificial intelligence, neural networking, emotional intelligence (the latter two adding up as it were to artificial intelligence), new media (social, personal, ubiquitous, convergent, disintermediated, intimate, addictive). Accordingly, perhaps we are not transitioning into the social

8. To be clear, global trade has a history of centuries if not millennia. It is not the same thing as free trade; the problem with free trade agreements is often not the trade, but the systems of governance that are written into them.

factory but into a world defined by new imaginations of energy and "raw materiality," an age in which data and algorithms are defining the possibilities and limits of life. And this is a world in which it is entirely possible to have capitalism without labor, but clearly not in the utopian way Marx imagined it.

We know that *there is a declining rate of mobility—economic, social and geographic* (and one might even add, cultural and political). These are no doubt connected, on the one hand, to many of the changes I have described already and, on the other hand, to what I will later call the affective landscape of the context. Consider the changing affective or emotional relations to spaces and places, to local communities and "home"; perhaps this is part of what separates the cosmopolitan from the traditional or parochial (if I may use these terms loosely for the moment and without any suggestion that the latter are somehow inferior, for in fact, U.S. urban intellectuals are often quite parochial). For the latter, contemporary times might be defined by the fear of losing one's home (literally) and one's community. From that perspective, cosmopolitan culture seems like an alien world, a world that celebrates homelessness, filled with people who seem to want to be citizens of nowhere, but claim to be citizens of everywhere (which gives them an uncomfortable relation to nationalism, and an apparent claim to universal correctness). From the other side, we might describe cosmopolitan culture precisely as a search for a different sense of place and space and with that, a different sense of home rooted in, e.g., communities of identity.[9]

We know that *many people do not understand the forces of change and do not feel in control of them.* This is not a new feeling—people have rarely felt in control of society or even their lives. What may be new is the particular way in which this feeling is articulated into a sense that one's country and one's locale are not only declining but deteriorating (which can be easily translated to "threatened,"

---

9. I am grateful to Allison Schlobohm for this insight.

as one seeks an external cause). In fact, again, this sense of malaise, of decline, demoralization, division and divisiveness, of defensiveness and defenselessness, of a growing decadence—this sense of a generalized judgment of negativity—is neither new in nor limited to the U.S. But one must take care, because although the "politics of feeling" has been crucial to the transformation of U.S. political culture since the 1960s, questions of feeling can easily place themselves beyond question or challenge. One has to ask how sentiments or affects are constructed and organized, harnessed and mobilized, and how they do and can be changed.

We know that *the population—and increasingly, many of its social, cultural and political institutions—are experienced as polarized and incommensurable.* People apparently do not want to socialize with people from the other side of the political frontier, and do not believe that conversation across the frontier is possible or even desirable.

We know that *this transition, this "creative destruction," which on the one hand has been happening over five decades, nevertheless feels like it has happened in a matter of years rather than generations.* This does not mean that the pace of changing is accelerating, or that contemporary life is somehow fundamentally characterized by speed. The sense of the rapidity of change is most certainly not new, although it has perhaps not impinged so much and so directly on individuals during their lifetimes. But it does seem understandable that people might feel a sense of disaffection, that this century is already broken, or heading to catastrophe.[10]

Of course, we know other things as well, but this will suffice; we need to tell better stories, stories that tell us some things we did not already know, stories that open up different futures,

10.   Chris Lundberg has suggested that one might locate here the reassertion of a muscular evangelical Christianity over and against Islam, as opposed to the new right's concern with moral decay (personal communication).

stories that, by embracing their own necessary incompleteness and fragility, offer themselves up as part of a conversation.[11] Such stories examine the forces and vectors of change, each with its own history, that are brought into and out of existence and that are constantly being reconfigured in different relations and with different intensities and priorities, to further particular possibilities of ways of being in the world with others. Such stories understand that history is not the product of conspiracies, but of struggles between and coalitions among conspiracies, some of them in opposition, attempting to articulate and deploy changes and forces of which they may not always be in control.

The only way to start is by trying to embrace as many of the details—structures, relations, strategies, experiences, projects, etc.—as we can, however contradictory they may be, to construct the context of what I earlier called a war of positions. I might assemble the following sites of contemporary struggle, recognizing that each can serve a variety of (tactical) functions since they matter in different ways to different constituencies and coalitions, and thus, consequently, that each crosses into several larger categories: economic matters such as job loss and insecurity, debt, economic inequality, taxation, regulation versus free market (e.g., health care, corporate behavior, energy and climate change, etc.); political matters such as government overreach and/or failure, minority entitlements and protections (immigration, race, gender, sexuality, ability) and national identity, the contradictions between rights, liberty and freedom; cultural matters such as education-truth-knowledge (versus?) religion (religious freedom, abortion, etc.), ethics of science (genetics, bio-engineering, artificial intelligence); "personal" matters such as privacy, surveillance and hyper-

---

11. What if one starts a conversation and nobody joins in. The "fact" is that such conversations are not only increasingly rare, but also increasingly difficult, partly for institutional reasons and partly for the reasons I shall describe later as the affective landscape.

exposure to messages and information; military matters such as international affairs, terrorism and the threat of nuclear war.

But the sense of contemporary struggles can also be understood in terms of multiple sites of experienced or lived crisis (although one cannot assume a simple one-to-one correspondence between the two lists as it were), which partly describes the discursive and political environment, and the modes of consent and engagement, surrounding the 2016 elections and around which a variety of temporary alliances and coalitions have been built. Here I might identify: a sense of increasing polarization (and "political correctness"), uncertainty about the lines between morality and politics, between certainty and common sense; changing ecologies of belonging and borders (raising crucial questions of sovereignty); unstable separations of public and private; growing mistrust of traditional forms and institutions of authority and cultural hierarchy; a collapsing sense of agency—of one's ability to shape the present and the future—whether in personal or social terms, and the resulting sense of precarity, despair and cynicism; and serious challenges to our assumptions about the relations between nature and technology, and even the nature of life, humanity and individuality.

The surprising thing is that, with a few exceptions, the sites of struggle and of lived crises are not especially new, although there may be something new about the ways they are understood and expressed, and the intensities with which they present themselves. Many of them have been around at least since the 1980s, some significantly longer, although a few have emerged in the last decade or two. However, their prominence and provenance, their place in the organization of concerns, and in fact, their power (whether ideological or affective) to configure the war of positions may well have changed. There are, at this level, a number of questions one might ask: how has Trump's victory been constructed—certainly not by consensus or consent? What is being signaled by the apparent collapse of the clear lines distinguishing the left and the right, as the leading agents of historical struggle? If it is, as it appears to be, the rule of a minority against the majority (an unpopular populism as it were, in which a minority assumes itself to be a majority), does Trump represent a political insurgency of some sort? Or is it the continuation of, or a blip in, a history that has been unfolding for the past fifty years?

These questions can only be addressed by moving to the level of conjunctural specificity, by contextualizing the current state of affairs. This involves identifying "tendential" or "organic" forces that operate across decades and even centuries, although their particular forms and expressions will change as they interact with one another and with more local, temporary developments. Such an understanding of conjunctural specificity seeks to identity what is old, and what is new, and how these inflect one another, in a particular contextual moment. I want, then, to describe two such forces, to tell two intersecting stories as part of that larger conjunctural analysis. The first locates the current moment in a longer history of the victory of conservatism. Consequently, I will recount, all too briefly, even schematically, a longer story[12]—one

---

12. There are many discussions of this history. For my own take (and extended bibliographies) , see *We Gotta Get Out of This Place: Popular Conservatism and Postmodern Culture* (London: Routledge, 1992); and *Caught in the Crossfire: Kids, Politics and America's Future* (Boulder, CO: Paradigm, 2005). Examples of more recent work include: Allan J. Lichtman, *White Protestant Nation* (New York: Atlantic Monthly Press, 2008); Anthony DiMaggio, *The Rise of the Tea Party* (New York: Monthly Review Press, 2011); Kim Phillips-Fein, *Invisible Hands* (New York: Norton, 2009); Corey Robin, *The Reactionary Mind* (Oxford: Oxford University Press, 2013); David Neiwert, *Alt-America* (London: Verso, 2017); Nancy MacLean, *Democracy in Chains* (New York: Viking, 2017); Robert B. Horowitz, *America's Right* (Cambridge: Polity, 2013); Chris Hedges, *American Fascists* (New York: Free Press, 2008); Michelle Goldberg, *Kingdom Coming* (New York: W.W. Norton, 2007). For important discussions of the rhetoric and communication strategies of the right, see Mike Waltman, *Hate on the Right* (New York: Peter Lang, 2014). For a

that stretches back seven decades—about the reconfiguration of the field of play defining conservatism in the U.S. since the Cold War.[13] The story of post-war conservatism makes apparent the fact that many of the most outrageous and disturbing actions of Trump's administration are not new, although perhaps more blatant and extreme (but that may be at least as much the result of new media possibilities as an actual change in political culture). But part of what is so odd about the present moment is precisely how much of this history seems to have been forgotten in discussions of the current conjuncture.

But this history leaves open a question: How was this victory of conservatism in general, and of Trump in the immediate moment, won? I do not think Trump's (and the Republicans') victory can be characterized as having been built on ideological consensus or hegemonic consent, although it was certainly more of a struggle over leadership than policy. Like hegemony, it is the rule by a fractured coalition but, unlike hegemony, that ruling bloc seems to be too contradictory to hold together, even among the fractions of capital. Moreover, there is no attempt to negotiate with other fractions and constituencies, to forge compromises around particular issues that could result in the construction of a dispersed and differentiated majority, built on a reorganization of the population around a vision of crisis and national purpose.

This leaves us with a problem: how was this history of victories that have consistently moved the center of political possibility to

---

discussion of contemporary evangelical rhetoric, see Christian Lundberg, "Enjoying God's death: *The Passion of the Christ* and the practices of an evangelical public," *Quarterly Journal of Speech* 95(4) (November 2009): 387–411.

13. I realize that limiting the story to the U.S. runs the danger of ignoring the ways that transnational forces have shaped the content and distribution of various conservative formations, as well as how these and other forces have weakened the very sense of an enclosed, isolated nation-state.

the right, and the latest victory, been accomplished? It has been constructed affectively, by articulating and organizing the field of emotions, passions, moods, matterings, etc., even though they are never completely in our control. I have written elsewhere about the affective conditions of possibility of the conservative victories of Reagan and G.W. Bush (and the general displacement of politics to the right) from 1980 to 2009.[14] In these earlier works, I characterized the dominant affective landscape as an organization of pessimism (compared to the organization of optimism that dominated from the 1950s into the '70s). But that landscape has changed rather suddenly and significantly since 2009, and I want here to describe the emergent landscape (of passive nihilism) that has shaped and enabled the present conjuncture.

There are other dimensions or tendential forces that form an essential part of the context I am trying to construct, although I will not discuss all of them here largely because they have been widely discussed by people more qualified than I. These would include, at the very least, stories about the history of post-war progressivism with its different practices and coalitions of struggle (as contrapuntal to the story of conservatism), about the transformation and complexity of the contours of economic and especially, capitalist relations, about the changing configuration of state policy and international and military relations, about the resurgence of religious and spiritual devotions, and the exponentially increasing influence of science and technology. Let me comment briefly at least of the first two of these, before turning to the stories that form the heart of my analysis.

Many commentators have talked about the supposedly extraordinary explosion of energy and the diversity of practices and movements that have risen up in opposition to Trump and recent Republican efforts.[15] But I would argue that these efforts also have

14. See my *We Gotta Get Out of This Place*.
15. The literature here is emerging very rapidly and is both prescriptive and descriptive. Here are just some examples: Becky Bond and Zack

to be understood as part of a longer history of the political forces shaping the U.S. since World War II, and that some of that popular energy has been deployed by the right as well. Still there is an important story to be told of the multiplicity of progressive social movements that have been helping to shape the contemporary political culture.

An adequate history of the progressive/movement left has yet to be written; it would have to describe and account for its ever-changing but often powerfully determining fragmentation and multiplicity; it would have to identity its multiple strategies and practices of protest, resistance, opposition and escape. It would have to locate the fractures and debates that have, for decades if not longer, both animated and constrained these movements: debates not only over prefigurative (participatory, horizontal) versus institutional (statist, vertical) politics; social justice (multicultural rights) versus economic, redistribute justice; oppositional politics versus the creation of alternative institutions, but also questions of the priority of issues, the symbolic value of styles, the effectiveness of tactics, the very meaning of "victory," the willingness or need for compromise, the relation between morality and politics, and the source of political authority (in identity, experience, knowledge, or commitment?).

Exley, *Rules for Revolutionaries* (White River Junction, VT: Chelsea Green, 2017); David Cole and Melanie Wachtell Stinnett, *Rules for Resistance* (New York: New Press, 2017); Charles Derber, *Welcome to the Revolution* (New York: Routledge, 2017); Joshua Holland, "Your guide to the sprawling new anti-Trump resistance movement." *The Nation*, February 6, 2017. https://www.thenation.com/article/your-guide-to-the-sprawling-new-anti-trump-resistance-movement/; L.A. Kauffman, *Direct Action* (London: Verso, 2017); Naomi Klein, *No Is Not Enough* (Chicago, IL: Haymarket, 2017); Jonathan Smucker, *Hegemony How-to* (Chico, CA: AK Press, 2017); Rebecca Solnit. *Hope in the Dark* (New York: Disruption Books, 2017), and more broadly, Sarah Jaffe, *Necessary Trouble* (New York: Nation Books, 2016).

It would have to identify the many formations and the various forms of alliance and unity that it has essayed, as well as its apparent inability or refusal to construct strategically effective and sustainable forms of victory and unity despite its occasional and important successes. It would have to consider the fraught relationships between the various movement lefts and the more formal party politics of (primarily) the Democratic Party (a much more precarious and hostile relation than the equivalent relation on the right). It would have to explain why this large and active movement (or movement of movements) has been losing the war for the political future of the country over the past sixty years even while one might argue that it is winning the battle for the cultural soul of the country. By that I mean that the state seems to have moved, slowly (although sometimes in rather startling leaps) and consistently toward more conservative and more pro-capitalist positions. The field of possibilities—economic, discursive and political—seems to have shrunk and to have been seriously reconfigured by the various alliances of new conservatives and capitalisms as they have responded both to social and economic changes, and to the challenges of the left.[16] Yet at the same time, the nation—and many of its forms of popular culture—is generally more centrist (at least) and sympathetic to many of the values and principles of the left.

In some ways, this story is crucial since politics is always shaped dialectically, through struggle, and much of the story of conservatism I will recount is defined in large measure by its response to the left, or at least to its perceptions of the left. I might here at least take note of some recent key moments, such as the 2003 protests against the U.S. invasion of Iraq, the 2006 Immigration marches, the election of Obama in 2007, the emergence in 2011 of the Occupy movement (which offered its own version of anti-elitism, in the figure of the "1 percent"), the emergence of Black

---

16. I have begun such an effort in *We All Want to Change the World*.

Lives Matter in 2013, the years of struggle that culminated in the 2015 legalization of gay marriage, and the slow but noticeable success of the movement to legalize marijuana. I chose these moments because they represent the diversity of issues, alliances, styles and tactics that have defined progressive politics.

The other "tendential force" that I want to comment on is that of the economy, particularly capitalism. We should remember two things: first, not all economic relations are capitalist,[17] and second, capitalism is a complicated and contradictory set of relations and practices. So we might begin this story by considering the contradictions and relations among its many fractions (finance, real estate and construction, energy and extraction, information technology, military, manufacturing, agriculture, media/entertainment/marketing, service), taking note especially of the growing domination of finance capital, the importance of knowledge economies, and the pervasive extension of service economies, which come together in the misleading, even deceptive, image of sharing economies. At the same time, the geographies of value have been rapidly changing, too often oversimplified in the image of globalization, which is really embodied in new forms of value-changes and mechanisms of logistics, and changing relations/contradictions between national and global regimes and economies, and the all-too-common elimination of competitive markets in the name of free market ideology. This almost necessarily would lead us to consider struggles, on the one hand, over various regulatory regimes (taxes, trade, monetary and fiscal policy) and, on the other hand, over various labor regimes (and the increasing impact of automation), both in the context of the growing intra- and inter-national inequalities (even while extreme poverty is being significantly reduced). Finally, any serious consideration of twentieth- and twenty-first-century capitalism would

---

17. See J.K. Gibson-Graham, *The End of Capitalism (As We Knew It)* (Minneapolis: University of Minnesota Press, 1996).

have to pay serious attention to the changing forms and powers of corporate agency and personhood,[18] including the changing nature of corporate culture. In the final analysis, the story of capitalism (only part of a larger story about economies) is inevitably a history of crises and struggles, and of the changing forms of political engagement deployed in and against the dominant forms of economic domination.

Let me return to my effort to tell a larger conjunctural story. Where exactly does this conjunctural story begin? The U.S. faced a series of cultural and political crises in the 1950s and '60s, to which both Johnson and Nixon were responses. The crises were the result of a series of damaging attacks from various emergent progressive (left) and conservative (right) formations, on the particular compromises that had been normalized as American liberalism. When this political crisis was articulated to a new crisis of accumulation in the 1970s that threatened the economic basis of liberalism, the U.S. was faced with the challenges of an organic crisis and hence, if you will, a new conjuncture. Since then, we can read U.S. political history as a seesaw between conservative and liberal settlements, from Reagan to Clinton to Bush to Obama. Although each proposed settlement changed the terms of the organic crisis to some extent, I do not think the fundamental configuration of the crisis shifted significantly. The question is: does Trump's election (and the emergent configurations of conservatism) signal the latest settlement on offer, or is it something else? Does the organic crisis that has driven U.S.

---

18. Corporations have increasingly taken advantage of the "corporate personhood" apparently established in 1886, *Santa Clara v. Southern Pacific*. More recently, *Burwell v. Hobby Lobby* (2014) seemed to grant corporations the protection of religious freedom, and *Citizens United v. Federal Election Commission* in 2010 granted corporate political contributions protection as free speech. See Andrew Davis, "Empires with/in/out the State: A conjunctural analysis of corporate sovereignty in the United States," dissertation, University of North Carolina, 2018.

political struggles for seventy years remain firmly in place, or is it being re-articulated in generally shared and understandable terms? Or is there something more? Are we seeing a struggle to construct a radically different organic crisis? Or even to deny the need for such a construction? Is the current conjuncture a continuation of or a significant break from the past fifty years or must we find the terms to see it as a negotiation between these options, as an effort (by different actors) to re-articulate the terms of any possible settlement?

PART II

In Search of the Conjuncture

4

The New Right

The story of post-war conservatism does not begin in the 1950s; it points back to older stories. The U.S. was built by slaves, and for a century, its economy and politics were crucially shaped by the institutions and demands of slavery. After the abolition of slavery and the Civil War, Reconstruction offered itself up as one of, if not the, defining moments of the nation. Viewed from the left, it was a momentous if temporary achievement. As Dubois was to write about it, Reconstruction offered the United States a new vision of its own possibilities, the opportunity to imagine the alliance of freed slaves and white workers. But the possibility was foreclosed by the combined efforts of political, economic and cultural forces and formations.[1] However, viewed from the right (up until recently, understood as the South), Reconstruction was the North intentionally humiliating the South, and just as importantly, an attempt by the federal government to impose its way of thinking and living upon the South through the appropriation of powers that rightfully belonged to the states. Here is the origin of extremist, violent white supremacist groups such as the Klan and the Redeemers.

The United States has a long, uninterrupted history of racism, although its forms and practices have changed, and often, at any one moment (and sometimes even in the same places), one can find different assemblages of these forms and practices. Thus, in

1. W.E.B. Du Bois, *Black Reconstruction in America* (New York: Harcourt Brace, 1935).

the U.S., at different times, race has been defined in biological, epidermal, ethnic and (various forms of) cultural terms; moreover, U.S. racism has also never been limited to "black" populations, but has been extended to other groups, so that at different times, different populations (including Italian, Jewish, Irish, Asian, indigenous and various white and brown people from Mexico and Puerto Rico) have been represented as black, or at least been on the receiving end of racism. One can also distinguish between forms of normalized, institutionalized and everyday racisms (including expressions of racialized grievances, without suggesting in any way that these are not destructive and offensive), white supremacisms (which oppose egalitarianism) and white nationalisms (which oppose multi-ethnic and/or multicultural societies). White supremacism assumes the inherent (necessary, universal) superiority of the white race over all others; it demands the absolute political and material subjugation of non-white populations (usually defined biologically and epidermally). And it assumes that this justifies all forms of racial violence including slavery and the racial cleansing (race war) needed to produce a white nation. White nationalisms do not necessarily embrace an absolute sense of superiority, which would justify subjugation and violence. They demand a racially pure nation, although how race and nation are defined may vary. They are certainly racist and they are often willing to accept and even deploy violence, but usually justify it as defending their nation from a dysfunctional social group who excuse their present anti-social behavior by appeals to their past mistreatment. But the forms of normalized racism can also end up in accepting and even legitimating forms of violence and profoundly consequential mistreatment. After all, the United States has a long history of military and police violence, aimed against indigenous peoples, slaves, union members, protestors, people of color, etc. as well as against the governments of other countries when felt to be in the nation's "interest."

Reconstruction also fueled feelings that are as old as the colonies. The U.S. has a long and deep history of not trusting, even hating, government. The U.S. Constitution was written to protect its citizens *from* the government—the classical definition of liberty. Perhaps this is partially justified by the fact that the United States has a long history of political and economic scandals.[2] The country also has a long history of paranoia, of imagining internal but more often external threats to its very existence, which have often been expressed in recurring bouts of xenophobia and anti-immigration politics, but also in a long history of anti-elitism and anti-intellectualism. Such sentiments have often gone hand-in-hand with over-the-top expressions of patriotism and nationalism.

A key moment in the history of such anti-government feelings, which fueled the emergence and shape of post-war conservatisms, can be traced back to the Gilded Age of the early twentieth century (which witnessed a country as politically and economically divided as our own moment), and which contributed in no small measure to the Great Depression; but the Gilded Age also gave rise to the Progressive Movement and the People's Party, which contributed in no small measure to FDR's "New Deal." The New Deal put in place the beginnings of a highly compromised social welfare state (much thinner and weaker than that of most European states) marked by profound moral surveillance, deep paternalism and patriarchy, and profound racism. It provided at best a thin safety net, though it also inaugurated a series of enhancements and extensions such as Johnson's War on Poverty. But the New Deal was also a spark that gave birth to the Liberty League, the first in a long line of "reactionary movements" seeking to preserve

2. Consider recent TV shows, like *House of Cards* and *Scandal*, which construct the State as little more than a site of corruption and crime, in which the major job seems to be making up and fixing the truth—giant steps beyond simple "spin."

the perceived legitimacy of the existing social hierarchy. In fact, since then, every Democratic president has had to face his own organized reactionary movement.

But the story of contemporary conservatism really begins with the Cold War and the solidification of "American liberalism." This is somewhat ironically the safest and most calming story that can be told of Trump's victory, for it then can appear to be simply the latest "settlement" in a long line of attempts to rein in the contradictions unleashed and articulated in the 1950s, '60s and '70s. Much that frightens people about Trump's actions are simply the further realization of a program, and forms of behavior, that have driven the New Right for seventy years. From this perspective, what distinguishes Trump's settlement is its peculiar version of populism (its anti-elitism that equates cosmopolitanism, intellectualism and identity politics) mobilized by a white nationalism, and a pro-capitalist, anti-globalization rhetoric. This is a populism that is neither of the left or right, neither urban or rural, neither class nor education defined; it is a populism that re-articulates the relationship between cosmopolitanism and parochialism.[3]

Conservativism has a long history in the U.S. One can, for example, point to the establishment of the Hoover Institute in 1919, and the American Enterprise Institute in 1943. Yet the Cold War posed new challenges to conservatives beyond the New Deal, and the emergence of the civil rights movement, the anti-war movement, the counterculture, and other "left" movements, which challenged the already "too far left-leaning" American liberalism of the Democratic Party and called a new version of conservativism into existence: rabidly anti-communist, deeply religious (i.e. Christian), strongly pro-capitalist (a big

---

3. It should be noted that in a sense, the success of populism was already presaged by the charismatic figure that Obama projected and his electoral success.

change for conservatism) and opposed to all "big" government (federal interventions) as forms of central planning and control, and therefore as antithetical to the fundamental American value of liberty. Part of conservatism's success may have been due to the fact that it was able to bring together multiple versions and sources of anti-statism, ranging from the anti-collectivism of the anti-communist right to the anti-regulationism of corporate capitalism, from the anti-Big Brother attitude of the libertarians to the anti-liberalism of the 1960s counterculture. Its founding hero was Russell Kirk,[4] who was convinced that the country was in the thralls of the liberal elite, which imposed its agenda over and against the people.

The story of this New Right (a fragile and changing coalition of conservative and capitalist fractions[5]) describes the development of a political movement committed to radically changing the culture of politics and the politics of culture. It was—and continues to be—willing to follow an uneven trajectory, to operate with compromise alliances, while holding onto its project, even as that project becomes more explicit, visible and totalizing with each victory. It is a movement that is systematic, strategic, patient and diverse (in terms of issues, priorities, practices and styles), so that, despite continual internal fractures and fights, it is driven by the need to continuously forge new "unities in difference." Many of Trump's most outrageous behaviors and policies can be located within the long-term trajectory to power of the New Right. But it is equally important to recognize that this history demonstrates a long-term strategic approach always marked by partial failures and incompletion. Yet each iteration of this conservative project

4. Russell Kirk, *The Conservative Mind* (Washington, D.C.: Regnery, 2001). The New Right that subsequently took shape ignored or rejected some of Kirk's positions and arguments, and these helped give shape and definition to an alternative, reactionary imagination of conservatism, in which Kirk is also a founding hero.

5. See Melinda Cooper, *Family Values* (New York: Zone Books, 2017).

goes further than previous ones; each one is bolder, continuing the (negative) effort to dismantle the dominant (New Deal, 1960s) liberal agenda. The New Right stands against the tide of post-war "liberal modernity" and offers a vision (or more accurately, a set of related but competing visions) of another modernity, a modernity defined by a social morality, a minimalist state and an empire of wealth.

In 1951, Bill and Vonette Bright founded the Campus Crusade for Christ, a key moment in what some have called the Fourth Great Awakening,[6] setting the stage for the union of (at least some) evangelical Christians, an emergent political conservatism and a globalizing free market capitalism. In 1955, William Buckley created the *National Review* as the voice of this new conservatism, aimed at countering the domination of the liberal press (sound familiar?). In 1960, he founded Young Americans for Freedom, an organization that was quietly building serious support on college campuses but choosing to remain largely out of public view. In 1964, the American Conservative Union was established.

---

6. Evangelical Christianity—a belief in salvation through grace and a personal relation to Jesus—has a long history, going back to the First Awakening in the religious revivals in England and the U.S. in the eighteenth century; the Second Great Awakening was linked to the temperance, abolitionist and women's rights movements. The Third Great Awakening, of the late nineteenth and early twentieth centuries, was associated with the social gospel, even as it stood in opposition to the relativism of historicist biblical interpretation and the secularism of Enlightenment science, especially evolution. It saw itself engaged in a modernizing cultural struggle for the very meaning of the nation, a struggle waged by identifying individual redemption with the national culture. Contrary to popular stereotypes, these movements were often largely middle class and urban. Fundamentalism, as an anti-modern, literalist interpretation of biblical inerrancy, emerged toward the end of the Third Great Awakening. The rise of the New Right is inseparable from the re-articulation of the politics of some evangelical churches toward the more conservative positions of Fundamentalists.

These groups, and the movement they figured, maintained their independence from the Republican Party, even as they tried, unevenly, to colonize it. They constructed a somewhat delicate relation between the movement and the party. One might say that their politics was to maintain one foot in and one outside of the party, and at each moment, they defended their own imagination of settlements capable of stabilizing the emerging organic crisis of the 1960s and '70s.

This new conservative movement saw itself as an umbrella organization, a relatively open and inclusive formation that did not have a single strictly defined creed. It was and continued for some time to be internally disparate, with its own forms and practices of internal organization. This was later embodied in Ronald Reagan's 11th commandment: Thou shalt not speak ill of any fellow Republican. Nevertheless, for decades, the movement did exclude—but only occasionally renounced—many extremist groups that are part of the history of right-wing populism and reactionary conservatism, especially white nationalists, white supremacists, neo-Nazis and fringe conspiracists, such as the John Birch Society, the Ku Klux Klan, and isolationists like the America Firsters, and amoral capitalist followers of Ayn Rand. Even more importantly, the movement saw itself operating with a long-term strategy. There were continued debates about how far to go, how quickly.

For example, many in the movement fought to win the Republican nomination for Barry Goldwater, against the mainstream—liberal, global capitalist—wing of the party represented by Nelson Rockefeller, who had, for example, proposed universal, single-source health insurance. Goldwater's supporters literally colonized the party as it were, attempting to win at all costs (so the practice was, inside the party, to attack your opponent even if you agreed with him).[7] Yet Goldwater had

---

7. See Rick Perlstein, *Before the Storm: Barry Goldwater and the Unmaking of the American Consensus* (New York: Hill and Wang, 2001).

begun to articulate an attack on the sophisticated cosmopolitan elites who thought themselves better than the "real" Americans living in rural counties and small towns that would become so important to both sides of the growing conservative movement. Actually, Goldwater was, in terms of conservatism, a deeply ambiguous figure who became a hero not so much for the New Right as for reactionary conservatism. Buckley refused to support him, ostensibly because the country was not ready for him, in that the movement had not had time to prepare and educate the country. (Buckley was right and Goldwater suffered a humiliating defeat, while Reagan, running on an agenda that shared some key elements, won 16 years later.)

That notion of thinking strategically, in the long term, was echoed over and over. Consider the following two "figures" of such political work. Buckley would often explain to audiences, after *Roe v. Wade*, that it might take fifty years to outlaw abortions, but it would be done. (He underestimated the time, but he was essentially correct.) Grover Norquist used a hitch-hiking metaphor to describe the movement's willingness to support candidates less conservative than they wanted: if you want to get to California, you might have to hitch a ride with someone going to Kansas City, and then another with someone going to Denver, or Las Vegas, etc. You might not totally agree with any one driver, you might not even like him or her, but they will get you a bit closer to realizing your agenda.[8] This sense of strategy and temporality defined the ongoing negotiation and the continually changing relation between the movement and the party for decades.

---

8. There is another strategy worth mentioning here: planned frustration. Focus on the inadequacies of public services and the desire for lower taxes (as an immediate increase in income, however small). Less government income means cutting services, which means increased deficiencies in public services, so further cuts in taxes and/or privatization seem reasonable.

But the new conservatism really took off in response to the left movements of the 1960s and '70s.[9] These are often, mistakenly in my opinion, divided into a political side (civil rights, anti-war, SDS, etc.) and a countercultural side (hippies, yippies, etc.), but these movements are better understood as a hybridized gathering together of many groups, issues, practices and styles. The Movement (of movements) was deeply divided, prone to internal dissent, fragmented, and, like its conservative counterpart, something of an umbrella assemblage. But unlike its counterpart, it was visibly and intentionally undisciplined, with little or no desire or capacity for a formal organization. This progressive movement was deeply divided over party politics and then, in 1968, the largest part (mainly led by the anti-war movement and not civil rights organizations) explicitly broke with the Democratic Party over Humphrey's refusal to commit to ending the war in Vietnam. That break no doubt played a big role in Nixon's victory. The Movement also deeply distrusted the mainstream media, especially the news, and often called it out for lying (and even tried to set up its own alternative media networks); at the same time, many of its tactics were designed precisely to take advantage of the media's modus operandi. In fact, many of the New Right's strategies (an affective politics, for example) and tactics (the use of the media, staged events, symbolic and performative protest, etc.) were appropriated from The Movement in different ways and measures in its rise to power.

Nixon and Vietnam had a major impact. Their imbrication played a significant role in the downward slide of trust in both government and media: both lied about the war over a long period

9. As I have said, the story of the New Right should be told alongside the story of what was sometimes called "The Movement," or the movement of movements, recognizing that the two very different, broad and opposing movements had very different temporalities and visibilities and very different relations to existing parties and party politics, although they shared some common criticisms of dominant liberalism.

of time. Vietnam changed the economic configuration of modern capitalism, when in 1971 Nixon decided to break the post-war Bretton Woods agreement and float the dollar, so that he could pay for the war through accumulating debt rather than by raising taxes. But Nixon did so much more, and it is at Nixon's feet that we can lay the most effective origin of the contemporary forms of polarization. Nixon was viewed with great suspicion by the new (anti-communist) conservatives—he did after all go to China, but he also set in place the three major strategies that have defined the rising popular acceptance of the new conservatism. First, and it was the most weakly enacted of the three, Nixon made it clear that he hated and distrusted the media, although he rarely confronted them head on. Second, more importantly, Nixon put in place the largely successful "Southern strategy," using racism to bring Southern white voters, who were traditionally aligned with the Democratic Party, to the Republican Party. But the most important strategy Nixon initiated was to describe the country as already polarized between a silent majority (which somehow never had to be defined) and the urban cultural and intellectual elites (often including the media), which his Vice President Spiro Agnew described, famously, as the "nattering nabobs of negativism": they criticized America and even criticized the patriots who celebrated America.[10]

Things happened quickly from then on and I just want to point to a few emblematic events. In 1971, the counsel for the U.S. Chamber of Commerce (later to become a Supreme Court Justice) William Powell wrote a memorandum, "Attack on American Free Enterprise System," which was a call to arms for capitalists and businessmen to come to the aid of the conservative movement to protect the economy from the left's attacks and its desire for socialism. In 1972, Phyllis Schlafly, an "activist and housewife" (who later became a constitutional lawyer) formed the

---

10. Trump has similarly attacked the very act of criticism.

Eagle Forum to defeat the proposed Equal Rights Amendment. In 1973, the National Right to Life organization was formed after *Roe v. Wade* legalized abortion. In that same year, the Heritage Foundation was created (with money from the Coors and Scaife families) as was the American Legislative Exchange Council (ALEC) (which has been profoundly important in writing legislature for both state and national conservative efforts). In 1975, the Trilateral Commission released "The Crisis of Democracy,"[11] authored in part by Samuel Huntington, which argued that there was a crisis of governance in the U.S., a crisis that was spreading around the globe, and at the root of that crisis was an "excess" of democracy. It was necessary, the report argued in classical conservative terms, to restore the prestige and authority of government institutions along with global capitalism. While it did put forth the beginnings of a conservative attack on democracy, it represents more of a transition point between mainstream Republican conservatism (whose platform in 1976, for example, continued to support the ERA) and the emergence of the New Right as a conservative movement not yet "in control" of the party.

But then the proverbial shit starts flying. The economic crisis presenting as "stagflation" sent economists and policy makers reeling; under Keynesian theory, this could not happen. The result was that the door was opened to a new political economy, embodied in the work of Friedrich Hayek and the efforts of the Mont Pelerin Society. Its opposition to state regulation (for anything other than creating and maintaining competitive markets, an idea quickly erased), planning and the sorts of state interventionism that had been unchallengeable since the New Deal, opened a new front in the battle against liberal modernity, even as it was eventually transmuted into supply-side, monetary

---

11.   Trilateral Commission, *The Crisis of Democracy* (1975). http://trilateral.org/download/doc/crisis_of_democracy.pdf

and free market policies. In 1977, the Cato Institute was founded (with Koch family funds) and the National Rifle Association began to engage directly against liberal politics. The success of the National Women's Conference in Houston (which presented its agenda for women's equality to Jimmy Carter, who was apparently too afraid to do anything with it) almost immediately gave rise to the "family values" movement, with groups such as Focus on the Family and later, the Family Research Council (1983).

In 1979, the Moral Majority was formed by Jerry Falwell and Paul Weyrich to give political voice to an almost entirely white "Christian Right" alliance that included some fundamentalists, evangelical Protestants, apocalyptic Christian Identity groups, and conservative Catholics; it was later replaced by the Christian Coalition in 1989, under the leadership of Pat Robertson, who had established the Christian Broadcasting Network as early as 1960. These organizations combined grassroots activism and electoral campaigning, especially around so-called "social issues" including school prayer, evolution, pornography, homosexuality and most intensely, abortion. These movements emerged alongside and fueled a shift in the popular images of white ethnicity, which were becoming more identified as an identity in its own right, especially as it was increasingly represented as both underdog and transgressive (e.g., the movie *Rocky*, 1976). The result was a new articulation of the effort to identify "American"—which is, after all, not an ethnicity—with the idea of (Christian) white identity, with its own particularity and its own politics of subjugation and victimage. This Christian white identity movement helped elect Ronald Reagan in 1980.

Roger Ailes and Lee Atwater changed the face of electioneering by compiling a database of single-issue voters,[12] and helping

---

12. I leave open the question of whether the fact that some people "explain" their support for a candidate or party based on some single issue should be taken as a sufficient account. For a discussion of Reagan as the first victory of the New Right, see my *We Gotta Get Out of this Place*.

to organize a campaign aimed at winning not an ideological consensus but affective consent to Reagan's leadership (and by proxy, his conservatism). Reagan's campaign was both a war of positions and a hegemonic victory that established what Hall called an "authoritarian populism." The coalition of forces he put together was immensely and deeply contradictory, including supply side and free market economists as well as economic nationalists, neoconservatives (who wanted to use U.S. military power to change the international face of the world by engaging in "nation-building"), the religious and moral right, and anti-government libertarians. This coalition was highly unstable and it forced Reagan to frequently compromise his own stated policies and promises. Additionally, Reagan's tenure in office was a constant flow of scandals and lies, which often led to a constant stream of jokes about Reagan's own intellectual deficiencies, but they seemed to have had no effect on his popularity or success—the Teflon president indeed.

With Reagan's victory, the conservative movement moved quickly and strategically to solidify and expand its position of power. The Federalist Society was formed in 1982 to transform the culture of law schools and the judiciary. In 1985, Americans for Tax Reform was born, and in 1988, Rush Limbaugh went on the air with his talk radio program. Throughout the decade, the New Right published a continuous flow of influential books by such authors as Charles Murray, Francis Fukuyama and Allen Bloom.

Still, following Reagan, the rush to conservatism seemed to slow down. The first George Bush was a bureaucrat, with no strong allegiance to the New Right. And then in 1993, the pendulum swung, not to the left, but to a right-center democrat from the South, Bill Clinton, who was perhaps even more pro-capitalist in his policies than Reagan and whose commitment to socially progressive politics was, at the very least, limited. Then the pendulum swung again with a new settlement—the second George Bush in 2001, a "compassionate conservative" who was aligned with and certainly sympathetic to the agenda of the New Right even if, in the end, he was perceived as having failed the movement. Yet Bush's advisor, Karl Rove, fueled the emergence of a politics of the base by emphasizing not only more local political struggles but also by using state referendums on social issues to increase voter turnout.

And it swung again in 2009 with Barack Obama, whom one might describe as a compassionate neoliberal, but was treated by many as a prophetic—almost messianic—figure of democratic populism. But this image of a pendulum is misleading, rewriting a commonly held assumption that U.S. politics always pulls candidates into the center. It might be more accurately described as a "turning of the screw," an intensification of struggles. We have been witnessing a particular mode of transition—an ongoing but uneven, highly strategic struggle across a range of issues and positions. And yet, Obama's victory was also the point of emergence of another more reactionary and, at least for a while, populist conservatism.

In the past decade, we seem to have forgotten much about these various settlements and the persons who stood in for them. Reagan and Clinton, but especially Bush, lied. In fact, it was during Bush's reign that the notion of the "big lie" became widely used—tell a lie that is big enough to be outrageous and repeat it so many times that people cannot remember when they had not heard it. Then it becomes true. We have forgotten Reagan's and Bush's ignorance and incompetence, which were often linked to various psychological diagnoses. We have forgotten especially Bush's attacks on science, his statement after 9/11 that people should go shopping, his "axis of evil," his attacks on the media (even as they regularly attacked and belittled him). G.W. Bush was Trump before Trump.[13]

---

13. I cannot help but think here of an old folk song from the 1960s, by Patrick Sky: "Reality is bad enough, why should I tell the truth?"

In the meantime, the country was becoming even more polarized, and practices of racism and racialization often played a central role. Rodney King's 1991 beating set off major protests and set loose new angers—on both sides—and the O.J. Simpson trial in 1994 went a long way in re-legitimizing public expressions of racism that had been silenced, even if only by the accepted norms of civility; the trial made visible the raced polarization of the population. Fox News premiered in 1996 as the outlet for a partisan conservative view of reality to oppose the domination of the liberal media, echoing William Buckley. The terrorist acts of 9/11 (2001) were taken up by conservative media in ways that set the stage for a more reactionary conservatism, whether that was their intention or not. They suggested that it was America as white, Christian capitalist culture that was in danger of becoming a victim. And this was a threat, according to G.W. Bush, not of criminality (like the so-called "drug wars") but of a military power, another nation albeit one that could not be defined in territorial or statist terms. The enemy was a non-state nation, which meant there was nothing left to define the enemy except its culture—or more specifically, its religion. (I shall return to this notion in Chapter 7.) Thus it was almost necessary that Bush renationalize the threat by locating it in Iraq. While Bush's new militarism might have given him an opportunity to address the failure of Vietnam and of his father's invasion of Iraq, more importantly, it set the country on a new terrain: a culture and politics of permanent war that has made the military into the most admired institution in the country.

5

The Reactionary Right

The inheritance of Clinton and Bush was a deregulated finance economy, eventuating in the debt crisis of 2007–08 and the Great Recession. Many on the left thought this was the beginning of the end of capitalism as we knew it (i.e., "neoliberalism") but they were wrong, as much because the left was unable, had no strategy in place, to use such a crisis to reconfigure an organic crisis. Stuart Hall said it was a crisis that would not fuse. I say it was a crisis that the left was not able to fuse, and that the right did not want to, at least not immediately, perhaps because Obama was the new president. The response to Obama seemed to absolutize the polarization of the country, no doubt based largely on the rising racism of the nation. The Great Recession and the Obama presidency—as well as Bush's failures and the apparent Republican Party's abandonment, under his leadership, of a truly conservative agenda, called forth the emergence or re-appearance of a populist version of a reactionary conservatism[1] in the form of the Tea Parties, aided no doubt by the attention of both the conservative and mainstream media.

The story of this more extremist vision of conservatism, often marginalized and existing outside of, or at least at the borders of, the Republican Party and even the movement politics of the New Right, is more difficult to tell because the lines that

---

1. While it has sometimes been called "old or classical conservatism," it is unlikely that such classical figures as Edmund Burke would have agreed.

delineate the movement are less clear. Its roots extend back to the anti-democratic sentiments of many of the Founding Fathers, who designed a system that privileged freedom as liberty, and that sought to protect the minority from the mob rule of the majority. It extends through the anti-Masonry movement of the 1820s and '30s, Andrew Jackson's presidency, the Know-Nothings of the 1850s, the isolationist (ethno-) nationalism of the America-Firsters, the "Farmers' Revolt" in the 1890s,[2] the various appearances of the white supremacist Ku Klux Klan, and the rabid anti-communism of the John Birch Society. Its post-war incarnation was sometimes called "paleo-conservatism"; its first post-war hero was Robert Taft, who lost the Republican nomination to Eisenhower (seen as a "liberal" and internationalist Republican) in 1952, followed by Barry Goldwater in 1964, and Pat Buchanan, who waged unsuccessful presidential campaigns in 1992, 1996 and 2000. Goldwater defined the affective tone of the movement: "Extremism in the defense of liberty is no vice, moderation in the pursuit of justice is no virtue." The capitalism he defended was that of small businesses, against the global capital that his opponent for the nomination, Nelson Rockefeller, represented. He rejected the Trilateral Commission report as an effort "to seize control and consolidate the four centers of power—political, monetary, intellectual and ecclesiastical—in the creation of a world-wide economic power."[3]

In the post-war years, this movement overlapped with the emerging New Right, especially on social issues and matters of religion. But it also diverged on several grounds. Paleo-conservatism practiced an explicit politics of resentment, scapegoating and white supremacism, so much so that it was

---

2. A movement opposed to the wave of Irish Catholic and German immigration, which became the American Party in 1855.

3. Barry Goldwater, *With No Apologies* (New York: William Morrow, 1979), p. 299.

often rejected by other conservatives as racist and anti-Semitic. Its fundamental appeals were populist, built on a sense of "the people's" declining cultural influence, economic security and political power, and it despised any hint of multiculturalism in favor of ethno-nationalism ("tribalism"). It rejected globalism (eventually including the New Right's neoliberalism) in favor of isolationism and economic nationalism. It favored a very limited view of natural rights (if it accepted them at all) as life, liberty and property, and a strict literalist reading of the Constitution. And its worldview was deeply conspiratorial. Although paleo-conservatism as a governmental strategy has largely disappeared from public view, it still exists in such institutions as the Rockford Institute, and through such spokespersons as Sam Francis (who died in 2005). Over the years, it has found even more extreme expression in a variety of neo-Nazi, white supremacist, and survivalist militia. This reactionary right has often pre-figured the possibility of an insurrectionary—civil—war, based on a politics opposed to the national government derived from states' rights, strict constitutionalism and white supremacism. But this politics of what I will call "reactionary counter-modernity" has resurfaced around the figure of Trump in several highly visible and effective forms. And perhaps even more importantly, these reactionary politics are increasingly re-inflecting the politics of the New Right into more extreme, absolutist and even violent positions.[4] But this developing relation has two further consequences: first, insofar as some conservatives resist the pull, there appears to be a civil war developing with the right. And second, even as conservatives are being pulled into reactionary politics, the reactionary right finds itself defending policies aimed at deregulating and strengthening global capital, a contradiction if ever there was one.

---

4. See the particularly frightening NRA ad, which comes within a hair's breadth of calling for a civil war: https://www.youtube.com/watch?v=PrnIVVWtAag

In 2009, the Tea Parties emerged from what appeared to be a spontaneous comment by reporter Rick Santelli on the floor of the Chicago Mercantile Exchange, although the movement has been largely funded by the Koch brothers. This combination of apparently spontaneous grassroots activism with corporate funding—"astroturfing"—is common among reactionary conservative groups. The Tea Parties comprised a de-centered, national movement of autonomous local groups that set their own agendas and tactics; the movement had no formal national leadership or organization, although there were several organizations that claimed to represent various coalitions, and several figures such as Sarah Palin and Ted Cruz who claimed to represent its politics. While it was, and remains difficult to gauge its support, polls at the time estimated support between 10–30 percent of Americans, most of them white (evangelical) Republicans.

The Tea Parties practiced a highly emotionally charged, populist, anti-elitist and anti-establishment politics, drawing heavily on the symbolic and performative tactics of the 1960s Movement; they took partisanship to a whole new level, hijacking the New Right's history and some of its strategies, even visibly breaking Reagan's eleventh commandment in the name of the twelfth: that shalt not compromise, making the refusal to compromise absolute. Many groups staged primary challenges against Republican candidates (accusing them of being "RINOs"—"Republican in name only") whom they believed were not sufficiently committed to small government, which they performed as a strict—literalist and originalist—constitutionalism (echoing the commitments of many elements of the Christian right), and economic policies (debt reduction and tax cuts) that would necessarily shrink government. Although publicly the Tea Parties usually eschewed socially divisive issues, many observers have argued that the Tea Parties were fueled by racism (derived from and articulated in their hatred of Obama) and their own defense of white identity as a victim of federal power. In the process, they redefined the very existence of identity as constituted by experience and feelings: whiteness is constituted as something experienced and its oppression is a matter of feeling victimized.[5]

Yet, perhaps most importantly, the Tea Parties saw themselves, perhaps only symbolically, as a revolutionary insurgency, as renegades who challenged the state and the "normal" practice of politics from both outside and inside the Republican Party. It was not just that the Republicans were not living up to their conservative commitments, it was almost as if the problem was that the Republicans were still committed to the practice of governance itself, at least on the federal level. Hence, the Tea Parties were not about taking over the Republican Party so much as holding it to the fire, sabotaging it and obstructing the very practice of government whenever it became possible, acting apparently without any fear of reprisal (partly the result of gerrymandered electoral districts that ensured their re-election). They were willing to shut down the government without any fear of electoral consequences. If Newt Gingrich was pilloried when he forced a government shutdown in 1995 and '96, Ted Cruz did it with impunity in 2013.

The Tea Parties exerted enormous pressure on the more "establishment" supporters of the New Right, pushing them to adopt a policy of complete and total obstructionism against Obama's agenda,[6] an expression of their hatred for Obama, both as a black man and as a popular liberal politician. In fact, it became more important to embrace and even augment the increasing sense of polarization than to solve the problems facing the country. They unashamedly put their hatred, their abandonment of any sense of

---

5.   In this, the Tea Parties unknowingly joined forces with fractions of the left that were similarly redefining identity and the politics of difference.

6.   This echoed the strategies Goldwater's supporters used to win the nomination.

political responsibility, and their rejections of the social norms of civility on public display, and the media make it all visible with little or no critical engagement.

The Tea Parties were, however, only the beginning of the story of the re-emergence of reactionary conservatism. I want to point to the emergence and, in some cases, the apparent legitimation (at least as defined by serious news coverage) of at least four additional reactionary formations. Too often, at least two of these (and sometimes the Tea Parties are also included) are grouped together under the sign of the "alt-right," a term proposed by white supremacist Richard Spencer in 2010 to describe a loose coalition of "identitarian" ("white nationalist") groups with diverse political agendas and practices. These groups reject the New Right Republicans, who have abandoned true conservative commitments out of fear, corruption and self-censorship. They argue that the old political identities—liberal and conservative, left and right—no longer work, even as they present themselves as a new kind of conservative (although in some respects their conservatism is very old). Consequently, they tend to want to construct themselves not as conservatives, who have not taken on the real battles, but as a "third position." Yet for the most part, they seem to define themselves more by what they stand against than by any well-defined vision of an alternative future. Still, I think a certain vision is operating, as I hope to suggest.

They assume that left/liberalism largely if not completely dominates and defines the U.S., not only in social and cultural matters (embodied in the liberal media-education complex), but also in political and economic policies. They reject egalitarianism and globalism as two of the foundations of American modernity. The former has defined the major terms of U.S. politics, placing unquestionable positive value on diversity and difference, even while arguing that such differences are only social constructions. The latter, combined with an economic theory that fetishizes growth, has resulted in a system that exports debt (hence the growth of finance) and imports unemployment.[7] For some of the populists among them, it is corporations that have undermined democracy.

Despite these common commitments, the label "alt-right" strikes me as self-serving: not only does it cover over the differences (e.g., differing loyalties to religion and the Constitution) but in the end, it serves as cover for the most hateful (neo-Nazi) versions of reactionary conservatism. And at the same time, I think, it does not get at what binds these reactionary fractions together. In fact, I think it is only by laying them out separately, trying to identify their differences, that one can see the frightening commonality operating in their political visions. The first two fractions are often associated with *Breitbart News* and hence, with Trump advisor Steve Bannon, and with bulletin board and chat websites like 4Chan. But Bannon is perhaps a more significant icon, for he figures an alliance amongst the various reactionary fractions, all of which advocates a move from an older reactionary politics, where values, jobs and community matter more than profit (to echo one of Bannon's heroes, Pat Buchanan) to an even more radical project.

The first fraction is perhaps the most peculiar. I will call them "post-libertarians." Although Allun Bokhart and Milo Yiannopoulos, in their widely read manifesto of the "alt-right,"[8] claim that they are largely young (millennial?), technologically committed libertarians—many were at some point supporters of Ron Paul—they have distanced themselves from libertarians as having failed to fight for the commitment to absolute liberty. Bokhart and Yiannopoulos describe this movement as "born out

---

7.   Hence the expansion of unnecessary service labor, education, prisons and the military as places to "store" unemployment, all of them racially structured in different ways.

8.   Allun Bokhart and Milo Yiannopoulos. "An establishment conservative's guide to the alt-right," *Breitbart News*, March 29, 2016. www.breitbart.com/tech/2016/03/29/an-establishment-conservatives-guide-to-the-alt-right/

of the youthful, subversive, underground" side of the Internet, what they call the "meme team" and what most of us call "trollers." Referring to their followers, Bokhart and Yiannopoulos claim in their manifesto that "Ironically, they're drawn to the alt-right for the same reason that young Baby Boomers were drawn to the New Left in the 1960s: because it promises fun, transgression, and a challenge to social norms they just don't understand." Comparing themselves to the New Left, the Merry Pranksters and the Yippies, these hacktivists and trollers aim to gain attention, disrupt, upset and discomfort people. And they do this all in the name of freedom. These post-populists are passionate, angry, frustrated and pessimistic, born as it were of insecurity. They are an educated vanguard for "low-information" voters, which might suggest something about their lack of faith in any democratic definition of politics. There is also, often, a certain "science fiction" ambience to their writing, and they often have close ties to (albeit as a somewhat distorted mirror of) the techno-utopians of *Wired* magazine, among others.

What are the politics of this formation? Some claim that these contemporary media anarchists do not care about politics; they just want to have fun—by sticking it to the boring farts who take themselves too seriously, who are too self-righteous, too complacent. They intend only to challenge and undermine such sentiments by humiliating those who embody them on the Web or in the media. It just so happens that such people are usually progressives/leftists. Many trollers affirm that the practice is largely affective, meant to celebrate its own insignificance and absurdity, disclaiming any relation to truth, precisely by revealing the insignificance and absurdity of the all-too-passionately held certainties of whomever or whatever is being attacked. Others argue that many trollers are only in it for the money and it just so happens that there is more money to be made by attacking liberals and occasionally, even up-tight Republicans, than conservatives or especially reactionary conservatives. Apparently, some were "disturbed" to learn that they may have contributed to Trump's electoral victory. Both these accounts seem ... unconvincing

They ignore the fact that the when trolling becomes political, in fact hyper-political (as with "Gamergate" in 2014,[9] or the false news websites), it is almost invariably linked to the reactionary right. These counter-cultural activities are almost always racist and misogynist, and it does little to claim that they do not really mean it. They adopt many of the discourses of white nationalism and "white identity," although their racism rarely slides into the more violent forms of white supremacism of the neo-fascists, whom I shall discuss in a moment.

But it seems to me, without meaning to diminish or ignore their reactionary racism and misogyny, that the real significance of this reactionary formation lies elsewhere. They want to drive people crazy, make them paranoid and unsure about what is going on, create panic and above all, chaos. And it is not only these young counter-culturalists who are defining this new form of (post) libertarianism; as I will argue later, such performances are apt descriptions of the actions of Trump and his administration. This is a different kind of politics, an anti-politics politics, a revolution against politics itself. And, we will have to ask ourselves, what is the politics of chaos?

The other reactionary formation often associated with *Breitbart News* and Bannon, has a direct connection to earlier extremist groups that were excluded from the New Right; it is or comes very close to neo-fascism, most clearly in the forms of white supremacism and anti-Semitism, arguing for the biological reality of difference so that the western culture they champion is necessarily a product of "the European [Christian] gene pool."

---

9.   Gamergate was an online controversy in 2014 involving misogynist attacks on women in the video-gaming culture. It was one of the first visible examples of alt-right trolling. See https://www.theguardian.com/technology/2016/dec/01/gamergate-alt-right-hate-trump

They are opposed to a multiracial and multicultural society, but at least some are more ambivalent about multi-ethnicity. Its participants and supporters, self-described "natural conservatives," demand homogeneity, stability, hierarchy, order and the familiar. They see culture as paramount, and believe it is in some way inseparable from race.[10] They tend to think apocalyptically, foreseeing the coming catastrophe (e.g., the race war), connect at least Bannon to Strauss and Howe's theory of cyclical history— each cycle always ending in catastrophe, with the contemporary U.S. rapidly approaching the "fourth turning."[11] Richard Spencer is this group's most visible media presence and, it is claimed that this formation is represented in the Trump White House by figures such as Stephen Miller, Sebastian Gorka and Julia Hahn.

Some people have claimed that the "intellectual" foundations of this new fascist, white supremacism, are to be found in the work of Julius Evola, which has had a sudden resurgence and popularity. Evola was an Italian fascist who eventually abandoned Mussolini as not having realized a truly fascist fascism (and so turned to German Nazism); he was a leading proponent of what is called "Traditionalism." Traditionalism sees fascism as a spiritual politics, offering up an almost pre-Christian vision of race and European identity. Rejecting Renaissance humanism and Enlightenment notions of progress and equality as dangerous lies, it calls for, as the title of his 1934 book suggests, *The Revolt Against the Modern World*.[12] And this revolution cannot seek to

---

10. Bokhart and Yiannopoulos align themselves with the attacks on cultural appropriation coming from some fractions of the left. They claim that their attitudes on race and immigration do not entail personal bigotry but a defense of tribal (white European) culture. They admit that their numbers include racists and bigots, but they "renounce" them as undesirables.

11. William Strauss and Neil Howe, *The Fourth Turning: An American Prophecy* (New York: Broadway Books, 1997).

12. Evola, Julius, *The Revolt Against the Modern World* (Rochester, VT, Inner Traditions, 1995 [1st English edition; original edition 1934]).

simply change or undermine or even escape the disaster that is modernity, it must, in Evola's words, "blow everything up." On the other hand, Bokhart and Yiannopoulos claim that these groups are really seeking a compromise with dominant liberalism that would allow conservative areas of the country to establish and live their own norms around issues of race, gender and immigration (a secessionist movement?).

Finally, I want to talk about two other, more recent and more intellectually oriented reactionary groups. I look at the first of these, who call themselves neoreactionaries (NRx), in part because they have not been very widely discussed outside reactionary circles, and in part because I think they make visible one version of the new vision that binds together the various formations of reactionary conservatism in the U.S. today. Neoreaction is an intellectual movement whose leading exponents are the pseudonymous Mencius Moldbug (computer scientist Curtis Yarvin)[13] and Nick Land (an English theorist who co-invented "accelerationism"). They did not support Trump (in fact, they rejected his election bid), do not identify with *Breitbart*, and do not think that their position is represented in Trump's actions. (I disagree with the last claim, although its presence is only in a hybridized form.)

NRx is a radically anti-Enlightenment theory of political history, written often in an ironic and intentionally confrontational style and existing solely online; it often reads like conservatism after postmodernism. It repackages some very old, reactionary conservative ideas into a ruthless critique of the Enlightenment (that often echoes contemporary left critiques). More accurately, it is mix of pre-modern, modern and postmodern elements that seeks to go beyond a critique of the establishment to a broader critique of modernity itself, and of the very practice of modern politics. NRx provides perhaps the clearest statement of the

---

13.   For the works of Moldbug, see http://moldbuggery.blogspot.com

contradictory nature of reactionary conservatism: committed simultaneously to modernist capitalism and pre-modern ideas of the politics of culture, nations and states.

NRx attempts to constitute a new communitarianism around the nation as a political community to be constructed by a new elite, based on their knowledge of the "common good" and using technological tools. It is anti-populist; it sees "the masses" as an ignorant rabble, a "howling irrational mob," and is completely opposed to democracy. While it strongly opposes the current (technocratic) elite, embodied in the mind-controlling, thought-suppressing activities of the Media-Academic complex, it does not reject elitism. Instead, it seeks a new elitism that would provide a radically new way of thinking about the world outside the terms of the Enlightenment. The Enlightenment is defined by three fundamental matters of faith: first, change is inherently good and progressive. To fulfill that commitment, the left always seeks the power to destroy the old order and construct a new one (in the end, always built on its own self-interest). Second, egalitarianism (and with it, democracy) is the fundamental goal, and to fulfill that commitment, the left seeks to expand and complicate the decision-making processes of the state as the bestower of rights. And finally, the first two demands are universal. But what this means is that a parochial dogma (which Moldbug traces back to Puritanism) is imposed on others. As Land puts it (in terms of modernity): "modernity was something done by people of a certain kind with, and not uncommonly to (or even against), other people, who were conspicuously unlike them."[14]

Although it opposes the Enlightenment as embodying a left politics, it describes itself as a third position, an alternative to what it sees as the largely futile attempts of a besieged, mainstream (read: New Right) conservativism, which is unable or unwilling to

14. Nick Land, *The Dark Enlightenment*. www.thedarkenlightenment. com/the-dark-enlightenment-by-nick-land/

renounce and escape the Enlightenment (largely for fear of being called racist, etc.). Being reactionary (as opposed to conservative) involves a commitment to order, stability and security, hierarchy and authority, defined not in political or social terms (as in previous reactionary formations) but in formalist terms. Consequently, Moldbug and Land then construct a set of oppositions. In the modern world, democracy and emancipation negate freedom and independence. The demand for equality and difference negates civilization as defined by a western pre-Enlightenment culture. The understanding of tolerance as the right to be heard (voice) negates a more fundamental understanding of tolerance as being left alone.

This provides NRx with its primary image of political struggle and subversion: freedom as exit or escape. Rejecting any notion of compromise with Enlightenment/modernity, they advocate or rather predict the inevitable "existential civilizational cataclysm," a "comprehensive crisis and disintegration" of the existing order. Democracy will destroy the very population it purports to emancipate. To quote Land again:

> By the time [modernity] was faltering ... in the early twentieth century, resistance to its generic features ("capitalistic alienation") had become almost entirely indistinguishable from opposition to its particularity ("European imperialism" and "white supremacy"). As an inevitable consequence, the modernistic self-consciousness of the system's ethno-geographical core slid towards racial panic, in a process that was only arrested by the rise and immolation of the Third Reich.[15]

Thus, while they seem to advocate some version of white nationalism, they do not support white supremacism, nor do they advocate for the possibility of a race war. Rather, in the very effort

---

15. Ibid.

to empower difference, Enlightenment modernity will bring about its own (racial) self-destruction. There is something very Nietzschean about their vision, as if we are living in the age of the last man, of passive nihilism.

The neoreactionaries have a number of visions of what comes next. Land calls up images resonant with Pat Buchanan's paleo-conservatism, which do not seem to challenge Enlightenment modernity: replacing representational democracy, downsizing of the state to its core functions (never specified), restoring hard currency and abolishing central banks, and finally, erasing macroeconomics to liberate the "autonomous economy," which he describes as "the real prize." But at other times, he seems to appeal to an older, even pre-modern order of self-reliance, honest industry and exchange, pre-propagandistic learning and civic organization.

But in between the lines of such banal visions and the warnings of a coming catastrophe, we can read something else: a call for less politics, for "anti-political governmental measures." This is where NRx connects with those movements that seems to want to blow up the system; it opposes the very practice of politics and the very existence of the state. Or so it seems, for in the final analysis, Moldbug calls for something quite radical and imaginative, if also horrifying in its audacity. His proposal, which goes well beyond the imagination of both authoritarianism and neoliberalism, calls for what might be called a "techno-commercial nationalism."[16] It is, in principal, quite simple: "Chartered companies are more likely to produce effective [i.e., profit-making] neo-reactionary governments than royal families," or one must add, democracy. The state should literally become a corporation which owns and can sell shares in the country, and it would function exactly as any corporation functions.

---

16. He calls it "neo-cameralism," based on Frederick the Great's rule of Prussia.

While NRx has been around now for over a decade and has, for the most part, rejected Trump and the recent "populist" insurgence, another intellectual formation appeared in 2016, largely in response to the long election cycle of 2016, gaining momentum after Trump's victory (and for some, Brexit as well); that is, they are *ex post facto* theorists of, or commentators on, the significance and possibilities of the new populism for conservatism. It is not so much about Trump—and there are different views about him within this group, many being deeply uncomfortable with his behavior—but about what some have called "Trumpism": what is it that his election represents? It therefore offers a second intellectual vision for a contemporary reactionary politics. While the Claremont Institute[17] has been the nurturing home for this work, it first appeared as a short-lived online blog (*The Journal of American Greatness*), in the first half of 2016, followed by *American Greatness*, an online website (https://amgreatness.com) and a new print/online magazine, *American Affairs Journal*.

"Trumpism" became publicly visible, as it were, with the online publication of "The Flight 93 election" in September 2016, by Publius Decius Mus (Michael Anton, who works for Trump's National Security Council). Publius criticized the establishment

---

17. The Claremont Institute, publisher of the *Claremont Review of Books*, was founded by Harry Jaffa, a long-time professor at Claremont College, and a student of the political philosopher Leo Strauss, and was revived in 2000 by Charles R. Kesler. It is often seen as the home of "west coast Straussianism." The east coast/west coast split between Straussians is usually traced back to an argument between Allan Bloom and Jaffa, over the role of "myths" in the social order, with the latter arguing that society was founded not only upon myths but upon some enduring, self-evident truths. Certainly, following Kesler's revival of the Institute, there was a greater sense of political urgency and of the need for intellectuals to be actively involved in the political struggle for principles (rather than abstract policy advice).

right (the New Right) and even the Claremont Institute (Kesler) for being overly optimistic, naïve and contradictory:

> To simultaneously hold conservative cultural, economic and political beliefs—to insist that our liberal-left present reality and future direction is incompatible with human nature and must undermine society—and yet to also believe that things can go on more or less the way they are going, ideally but not necessarily with some conservative tinkering here and there, is logically impossible.[18]

For Publius, the times are desperate—we are "headed off a cliff," "caught in a tidal wave of dysfunction, immorality and corruption." Even worse, "the deck is stacked against us." We should feel more desperate and act accordingly. Hence, the analogy to the doomed Flight 93, during the attacks of 9/11, when passengers stormed the cockpit, crashing the plane rather than allowing it to crash into the Pentagon. "If you don't try, death is certain … a Hillary Clinton presidency is Russian Roulette with a semi-auto. With Trump, at least you can spin the cylinder and take your chances." Publius did not particularly like Trump, but saw him, not simply as the lesser of two evils, but as a necessary evil, a "vessel" who, in rejecting political norms and pieties and establishment elites, opened the possibility of a new conservative movement. *American Greatness* describes this "next generation" of American conservatism as a "refounding" of a uniquely American conservatism, emphasis on the American.[19]

---

18. Publius Decius Mus, "The Flight 93 election," September 5, 2016. www.claremont.org/crb/basicpage/the-flight-93-election/
19. Editors, "Our declaration of independence from the Conservative Movement," July 21, 2016. amgreatness.com/2016/07/21/declaration-independence-conservative-movement/

This new conservatism is aimed against both the left and the right. Trumpism generally sees the liberal/left as ascendant, even in control, and assumes that it has been in that position since the end of Reagan's reign. It is defined by the rule of expertise which began when Woodrow Wilson brought his experience governing Princeton University to the federal government. Even worse, this governmental meritocracy is fueled by a disastrous education system which functions largely to indoctrinate young people into a new dominant force (a new McCarthyism) of identity politics and political correctness (which Kesler describes as "a new ugly stage in liberalism").[20]

Both establishment parties have accommodated to this politics, and neither is capable of addressing the most pressing problems facing the nation. Republicans and the New Right have failed to allow conservatism to develop as times have changed. Conservatism has been reduced to a checklist of inconsistent and incongruent policies—the "fusion" of corporate capitalism (consumerist individualism, neoliberalism, financialization, globalization) and social moralism. Trumpism often suggests that such versions of capitalism are against the national interests, and that the culture wars are over—and the left has won. Hence, for the most part, Trumpism refuses to advocate any partisan set of policies, since it is entirely a matter of principles.[21]

But this means that their rejection for the New Right is even more scathing: as *American Greatness* puts it, the New Right was "founded on principles that are either insufficient or in conflict with the timeless principles of the American Founding." And

---

20.   Charles R. Kesler, "Trump and the Conservative cause." *Claremont Review of Books* 16(2) (Spring 2016): 10–16.

21.   They will sometimes claim to have rejected partisan politics, rendering both right and left irrelevant, to offer a vision of a new "radical center." Against "ossified intellectual orthodoxies" that have led to the degradation of political discourses, Trumpism offers a new foundational political discourse.

American Affairs continues: "The essential task is the redefinition of the American people's distinctive interests in the present, and their unique hopes for the future."[22]

The task then is to reassert—against the left—the founding principles of the great American experiment at constitutional government, affirming the political sovereignty of the people. Trumpism in fact synthesizes two distinct commitments: on the one hand, the self-evident truths of the Declaration and the Constitution—"a universal standard" of equality and justice, and the rights that follow from these. And yet, on the other hand, these are offered "on behalf of one people in one place."[23] It is this combination of nationalism and popular sovereignty that defines Trumpism, although these may at times be in contradiction. Publius, for example, does suggest that re-establishing such sovereignty may require a bit of tyranny—"more control and less freedom."

Nationalism demands that politics is only justified in terms of what is good for the nation, what preserves the American way of life (culture), what preserves the body politic and enables it

---

22. Editors, "Our policy agenda," May 2017. https://americanaffairs journal.org/2017/05/our-policy-agenda/

23. "Our declaration". Of course, many on the left would agree to these principles but perhaps cringe at the thought of limiting them to a single nation. This particular contradiction is elaborated in Ofir Harvey and Yoram Hazony, "What is conservatism?" May 2017. https:// americanaffairsjournal.org/2017/05/what-is-conservatism/ They argue that the New Right and other so-called "conservatisms" built on notions of universal rights are actually forms of liberalism, following upon Locke's theory of universalist rationalism and an axiomatic politics. They contrast this with a true conservatism that is built on a kind of pragmatism, what they call "historical empiricism," which derives politics and law from historically changing national character, historical experience. It attempts to figure out how to adapt customary and traditional laws to present circumstances. As a result, for example, they argue that the Declaration of Independence is liberal while the Constitution is conservative.

to flourish.[24] This explains why Trump's nationalist agenda finds some support. He "takes the right stance on the right issues": immigration and secure borders,[25] trade, jobs and economic nationalism, and an America First foreign policy.

But this nationalism is only possible when tied to populism as the contemporary form of political sovereignty, which is the true American founding principle (apparently displacing any mention of democracy). Thus, "American greatness" is only achievable by the "virtuous action of the sovereign people" rather than the actions of experts. As a result, "a diligent attention must be paid to the opinions and interests—expressed or implied—of the American people in its totality and as it actually exists."[26]

I cannot help but note the difficulty, even the contradiction, that is constitutive of the synthesis at the heart of Trumpism. The question is, quite simply, who gets to define the nation, its culture, and the conditions of its greatness? Obviously, the people. But then, who are the people? Various authors will acknowledge that "the people" is not a simple, pre-given and permanent category; "the people" has to be made just as the American culture has to be defined. The founding principles defined above, even articulated into the present circumstances, do not guarantee in advance the answers, but Trumpism's nationalism does seem to simultaneously deny and embrace an exclusionary concept of the American people, potentially linking it to the racisms and xenophobia of other reactionary formations.

Some of this complicated history of conservatism—and the shift from the New Right to the new Reactionary Right—is visible in the changing ways in which "political correctness" has

---

24. They do sometimes acknowledge that this might open up to different understandings of the nation, but this is usually quickly glossed over.
25. Publius asserts that a nation that opens its borders, that supports mass immigration, is a civilization that wants to die. But that is not the history of the U.S.
26. "Our Declaration."

been taken up and deployed throughout the rise of post-war conservatism; in fact, it has been an essential element in the construction of changing anti-elitist appeals. The term originated in the left in the 1960s, as a sarcastic insult of a comrade who was being too rigid, too morally pure, too self-righteous. The right appropriated it in the 1990s as part of a larger, very well-funded attack on universities—think of Bloom's *The Closing of the American Mind*, Kimball's *Tenured Radicals* and D'Souza's *Illiberal Education*. These attacks were responding to real changes in the universities—calling the "canon" into question, giving more attention to questions of the social, political and epistemological effects and expressions of power, the creation of new disciplines around such questions—in the name of a supposed defense of European Enlightenment culture and education. But "PC" quickly became an accusation that the university left was enacting a "new fundamentalism," which was intolerant of disagreement and actively silenced other voices (in a very neat reversal of the left's accusations of the right, and the liberal mainstream). But then, something shifted. PC was used to describe not only intellectual elitism, but multiculturalism, understood as a politics that denied the desirability or need for a common culture or creed in the U.S. Such concerns seem to matter more for reactionary conservatism than the New Right. Earlier images of welfare queens were replaced by images of spoiled, self-entitled, whining minorities, thus cementing an anti-elitism that equated intellectual elites and "identity" activists. As both university and activist politics became increasingly personalized, increasingly a matter of "feeling" (safe), and increasingly a struggle against "privilege," reactionaries were able to combine the two historical images—of left fundamentalists and whining activists and turn it against both liberals and progressives (and to effectively elide the differences between and within these political positions). The dominant radicalism of universities and the dominant liberalism of the media became the representatives of PC, attempting to silence Trump, but he heroically battled them—demonstrating his energy, virility, potency, all captured in the exuberant, over-the-top presentation of his dystopian diagnoses and utopian promises, and all wrapped up as defining his white masculinity—and eventually defeats them.

With this historical context in place, let me reiterate my claim that Trump's victory was neither as simple nor as unprecedented as it is often said to be. Most of the behaviors that Trump's critics disparage are a continuation, even if more extreme, of practices that marked the rise of the New Right in the past fifty years: racist appeals and practices, anti-elitism, anti-intellectualism (anti-expertise, anti-science), the use of lies repeated, the practice of an affective politics ("Make America Great Again" is another empty but highly emotionally charged statement, like Reagan's "morning in America" or Bush Sr.'s "a thousand points of light"), the practice of making statements, promises (of actions, of presenting future evidence, etc.) and predictions that are never realized or fulfilled (but apparently simply ignored, denied, or erased from collective memory), the denial of responsibility or its projection onto other—external—sources. We should not forget Bush's lies including those about WMDs, the lies used to defeat Kerry, the Obama birther lies (which Trump finally renounced in September 2016 and then blamed on Hillary and which, apparently, many Americans still believe), the lies about the Clintons, the lies predicting the benefits of the "new economy" or the horrors of Obama's economic or health care initiatives, the list goes on and on. No doubt, Trump's campaigns (and continuing rhetoric and actions) seem to take many of these practices to new levels, but these may be the result of the changing media environs, and Trump's ability to work with them.

But that is not the end of the story. Trump is not simply Reagan or Bush on steroids. He has added the constituencies, voices, practices and projects of the reactionary right, and these additional elements mark a significant shift, even if their presence in his administration turns out to be only temporary. Perhaps that is why even the possibility of impeachment and a Pence presidency (which should terrify the left) seems like a reprieve, and perhaps it is why G.W. Bush can be—or at least can be imagined to be—rehabilitated in the face of Trump. It does feel like something deeper, something about the problem space, is changing, that this is a shift in what one might figuratively call the tectonic plates. It does feel like the terms of political power and struggle, affective sociality and hope, and epistemic consensus and dissensus are changing, that the field of political possibilities and imagination has expanded in frightening ways. So however much it looks like the next settlement, we need to take seriously the possibility that something else, something more, is going on. But we should not assume in advance that we know what it is, or where it might—and I emphasize *might*—take us.

If we do not then assume that Trump is simply the latest settlement in a long and developing shift toward a conservative politics tied to a free market capitalism, then perhaps we must consider the possibility that he has opened up a different direction and another possible future. If, as I have suggested, the war of positions has remained relatively unchanged, Trump's victory may signal an as yet undeveloped response to an as yet unarticulated set of changes and challenges. As I have said, I believe it is a moment in which the old is dying and the new cannot yet be born, so that what we are witnessing are the morbid symptoms of an ill-formed transition. It is these symptoms that we must understand rather than take for granted, for they are precisely not only the sites of potential struggle but, in some cases, possible openings into different futures.

Unlike previous unstable "ruling blocs," there seems to be little or no serious effort to construct any sense of (hegemonic) unity among the various capitalist, New Right and reactionary fractions. The space of administrative policy and discourse appears to be simply distributive and contradictory, and it is allowed to remain that way, with no well-defined doctrines or ideology to drive it forward. The actions of the state have become chaotic, well beyond the haphazard quality we might expect from a new and inexperienced president. It is easy to dismiss this by saying that Trump does not know what he is doing, that he is stupid or ignorant, or that he is mentally unstable. We should remember that we assumed previous conservative presidents were ignorant or crazy, and it did not get us very far in terms of either understanding what was going on, or developing effective strategies of opposition and progressive transformation. What if we assume that the chaos is both a result of the very nature of the ruling bloc and a desired effect on the part of at least some elements within it?

6

Affective Landscapes

But is that all that is new in the present conjuncture? Is that the only field of battle as it were? To say, as I have, that many of Trump's behaviors repeat older behaviors, even if they also inflate them, is not to say that they are the same. For as I have tried to stress, it all depends on the context, on how they are made to respond to and express the context in which they now operate. I have tried to describe one dimension of that context in terms of the resources offered by a political history and the ways Trump—perhaps unintentionally—has assembled a hybrid conservatism. But just as importantly, there is a deeper context, a condition of possibility not only of the particular configuration of conservatism and the chaos of Trump's administration, but also the ways people experience whatever is going on, and the ways they can embrace, ignore, or resist the event of Trump and the future it promises. This is what I have called the "affective landscape."

As I have said, affect defines the various organizations of intensity and feeling that give texture and a sense of lived reality to our lives. An affective landscape describes a complex social way of being in the world, a densely textured space within which some experiences, behaviors, choices and emotions are possible, some "feel" inevitable and obvious, and still others are impossible or unimaginable. It defines what is allowed and what is forbidden. And it is where the struggle to make new and emergent experiences livable and knowable is carried out. To use an inadequate metaphor, an affective landscape is like a fog in which one can only see and move at the tempos and in the directions allowed by the specific distributions, directions and densities of the fog itself. But they are not simply the background against which human sociality and agency are enacted; they are its active conditions and expressions, saturating and determining the limits and possibilities, the rhythms and patterns of social experience. Affective landscapes are what hold the world together by constituting a sense of unity and sanity.

The affective landscape is not only a crucial chapter in the story I am trying to tell, but also a key element in any calculation about how to change the story. Political possibility lies somewhere in the space between understanding how people do feel and imagining how they might feel, and it depends on figuring out how such feelings are made, organized and changed. Do we know what people feel today? What matters to them? What do they care about, and what they are willing to fight for? Do we understand their rage, fears, uncertainties, anxieties, hopes, desires?

In any conjuncture, there may be multiple, overlapping—reinforcing and even contradictory—affective landscapes, some residual and disappearing, some mainstream, and some emerging and still precarious. Moreover, any affective landscape can be articulated to a variety of political positions, allowing it to function simultaneously as dominant, oppositional, or alternative. For example, in the contemporary U.S., I might describe two residual organizations: an organization of optimism left over as it were from the 1950s and '60s, lived differently by a normative white culture, a youth-defined oppositional counterculture, and various minority cultures, and a more recent and still powerful organization of pessimism that arose in the 1970s and '80s. The latter nurtured and enabled the rise of both the New Right and a revitalized prefigurative politics of the left. But increasingly, the present moment is being shaped by what I call an organization of passive nihilism, which has been emerging and gaining strength since the turn of the millennium. I believe that this affective landscape is significant not only as a dimension of the current conjuncture—on which significant political work is engaged (e.g., the right's transformation of anxiety into resentment)—but also as the condition of possibility of the realignment of political positions and the reconfiguration of political culture, so that what was old (e.g., appeals to catastrophic and apocalyptic endings) can be made new.

Every affective landscape is itself a complicated assemblage. Structures of feeling are the components and expressions of an affective landscape, translating it into moods, defining the tonalities of our behavior, and mattering maps, defining the forms and sites of investment and caring, of attachment, attraction and distanciation. Structures of feeling define ecologies of belonging and possibilities of mobility. Each structure of feeling is itself a point of articulation between what is already known and experienced, and the emergence of new experiences that cannot yet be expressed and therefore remain unknown. If an affective landscape is a configuration of structures of feeling, then any structure of feeling can belong, even simultaneously, to different landscapes; and any landscape may be configured, even simultaneously, in different ways (i.e., the relations of structures of feeling within a landscape—their proximity, interpenetration and mutual determination—may vary at different social sites and for different constituencies).

I want to describe, however briefly, four structures of feeling that comprise in part the emergent organization of passive nihilism, recognizing that each has its own history (so that some extend far back in time, while others have only just appeared): (1) affective autonomy, expressed as hyperinflation and fundamentalism, which can almost seamlessly slide into what Henry Giroux has called a "culture of cruelty,"[1] (2) anxiety and hyperactivism,

---

1. See Henry Giroux, *America at War with Itself* (San Francisco, CA: City Lights, 2016), and Henry Giroux and Brad Evans, *Disposable Futures* (San Francisco, CA: City Lights, 2015). Also see Giroux's many excellent columns on www.truth-out.org

(3) sociality as personalization (narcissism), and (4) temporal alienation.

Affective autonomy describes the growing sense of a separation between what matters and how it matters on the one hand, and its actual value or content. It is the result of the proliferation of … well, everything, and the resulting sense of endless proliferation and chaos, across many domains—including knowledge, morality, culture, taste and politics, combined with the deconstruction of every standard by which one's choice can be grounded and justified. All that is left is the simple fact of the choice itself, that is, the fact that one has chosen to make an investment. In the face of an unavoidable relativism, the only ground for differentiation is affective, making the sorts of bubbles we descry almost inevitable. In a sense, this is the full realization of a process that began much earlier (some might even say it is the result of processes of mass commodification that began in the early twentieth century), in which, e.g., stories about tyranny and democracy, violence and charity, can be interspersed with advertisements for luxury goods, or claims that "American independence begins with …" whatever corporate product is being sold as radically innovative today. Facing the inability to judge the comparative value or merit of anything, the "reasonable" response seems to be to treat everything equally, or at least with equal suspicion, and to refuse to seriously invest in any one option over the others.

Every claim, every opinion, every choice has to be taken equally seriously or not seriously at all. The world is flattened out and the only way that anything can matter is with some degree of irony or cynicism. Or on the other hand, if an investment in something cannot be justified by its worth or truth, if there is no real basis for choice, then only the intensity of commitment itself can justify the choice. One is right about something because one is passionately committed to it. The quantity or intensity of the investment is what guarantees its validity, independently of any content. The power of will itself is all that defines truth, success and righteousness: "Where there's a will, there's an A." Sheer effort or desire is what matters, not competence or merit. Everyone can succeed and if they do not, it is because they did not commit with enough energy and fervor. Failure is the result of a lack or quantitative deficiency of commitment.

Affective autonomy is also the result of an increasing self-consciousness. Marx described ideology as "people do not know it [what they are doing], but they are doing it." Sloterdijk argues that in the contemporary world, people "know very well what they are doing but still, they are doing it."[2] This has profound consequences for political struggle, for it means that people are increasingly aware of the contradictions that define their common sense, and they have learned to live comfortably with them. Gramsci's image of a popular politics that enters common sense to prize apart the contradictions becomes increasingly irrelevant when the grounds of critical judgment have disappeared.

In the past decades, this affective autonomy has taken the form of "hyperinflation," a demand for affective exaggeration, in which there are only two possible valences of affective judgment. Everything has not only to serve its purpose well, it has to be great, the best, the biggest. Or the worst. But hyperinflation can also make the unimaginable into the normal and mundane (e.g., the overload of shocking tragedies). Everything becomes too emphatic; nothing can matter unless it is followed by an exclamation point, and everything sounds like it is followed by more exclamation points than one can count. Every movie is one of the best of the year, every car is rated number one, every brand is the best-selling, everyone should feel like a *billion* (didn't it used

---

2. Karl Marx, *Capital*, vol. 1, chapter 1. https://www.marxists.org/archive/marx/works/1867-c1/commodity.htm. This is also sometimes translated as "They do this without being aware of it." Peter Sloterdijk is cited in Slavoj Žižek, *The Sublime Object of Ideology* (London: Verso, 1989), p. 33.

to be just a million?). Designing the latest new model of a car is equated with Einstein's discovery of relativity; a single instance or image becomes the key to the universe; purchasing a new commodity recreates the courage of a war hero, and a single act of censorship becomes proof of fascism.

Hyperinflation almost inevitably becomes fundamentalism, in which any investment must be held absolutely, with absolute certainty. Any statement or action must be enacted with an intensity that is so over the top that criticizing it, or even doubting it for a moment, becomes impossible, unthinkable. Every claim becomes indubitable because even a moment of doubt or humility opens one up to the dangers of failure and even worse, of humiliation.

But hyperinflation and fundamentalism have a more sinister side: they have, in the past decade, taken the form of a popular fanaticism,[3] which constructs one's fundamentalist position as under attack, and one's limits as the result of victimage. In fanaticism, my choice is not only certain and absolute, but the only possible choice. And the only acceptable outcome is complete and total victory; anything short of that is failure, which is simply never acceptable. The world is completely constructed in binary terms, and the result is an absolute sense of partisanship that saturates every aspect of life on one or the other side of a frontier. There can be no compromise, because the other side is by definition evil. And if one cannot achieve victory, however it is defined, if one fails, it must be that one is a victim of external forces that oppose one's righteous and well-deserved goals, like the government, or liberals, or those "minorities" calling for "social justice." If others who do not share our commitments achieve what we perceive to be our just desserts, then it must be that they are being helped by those who oppose us, since, by definition, they cannot have earned the right to whatever rewards they have won. Those forces that oppose us, those groups that claim what we rightly have earned,

---

3. See Alberto Toscano, *Fanaticism* (London: Verso, 2010).

96

can only be understood as evil. And that evil cannot be mundane and ordinary; it must be absolutely negative. Obamacare is not just a mistake—it is the new slavery or Nazism. And Trump … at the very least, we should consider that those who oppose Trump are caught up in the same affective structures of autonomy, fundamentalism and, just maybe, even fanaticism.

Fanaticism puts in place a paranoid economy of superiority and inferiority, of good and evil, of the deserving and the undeserving. Such affectivity refuses to grant any space or legitimacy to the other side (cutting across politics, culture and knowledge). The inevitable resulting feelings of victimage find expression in what Henry Giroux has so brilliantly documented as the culture of cruelty that has taken over the affective political life of the nation.[4] Feeling victimized ends up in expressions of resentment and rage, enacted with varying degrees of affective and physical brutality and violence, aimed at "the enemy," whether it be individuals, groups, institutions, or even some anonymous other. These have become "everyday" forms of personal and collective action, ranging from psychological acts of bullying, shaming, humiliation, contempt and intimidation (e.g., trolling) to the physical infliction of suffering, including neglect, impoverishment, incarceration and murder. This is a culture that normalizes public viciousness, aimed at anyone or anything thought to be impeding one's own

4. This culture of violence and cruelty can also be inflected to the left, although I say this without any necessary judgment of the tactical thinking here. I have in mind some of the rhetoric and actions of re-emergent and sometimes violent antifascist groups ("Antifa"). See Alexander Reid Ross, *Against the Fascist Creep* (Chico, CA.: AK Press, 2017); Mark Bray, *Antifa* (Brooklyn: Melville House, 2017); Wes Enzinna, "This is a War and We Intend to Win," *Mother Jones* (May–June, 2017) www.motherjones.com/politics/2017/04/anti-racist-antifa-tinley-park-five/; Natasha Leonard, "Anti-Fascists Will Fight Trump's Fascism in the Streets," *The Nation*, January 19, 2017, https://www.thenation.com/article/anti-fascist-activists-are-fighting-the-alt-right-in-the-streets/?print=1

success. While many of the stories about Trump focus on feelings of resentment, I would suggest that the roots of the resentment and rage lie in the terror of the humiliation of being a victim. One avoids the humiliation of loss and victimage by humiliating the other, by diminishing their status and capacity, destroying their sense of pride, reducing them to a lower state of being. To thus mortify another—and to take pleasure in it—is to assert that one is not a loser or better, that one is not supposed to be a loser (but the other side cheats as it were). In the final analysis, humiliation is the very negation of empathy as a necessary condition of human communication and social bonding. It is beginning of the increasing violence of contemporary life, for it is always in the eyes of the beholder (as opposed, e.g., to shame). One might say that the structure of feeling I am describing contextualizes the story of resentment, enabling one—hopefully—to understand what is specific about its contemporary forms, rather than just taking its affective reality for granted.

The second structure of feeling constitutes the immediate tone of contemporary experience as an almost omnipresent, historically specific sense of anxiety.[5] Anxiety disorders are now the most frequently diagnosed, and intolerably high levels of anxiety have become the norm of American life. Here anxiety is not quite the same as (but not completely separable from) a sense of risk, danger and insecurity. Unlike fear, which always has a referent, even if it is invisible, absent, or displaced into the future, and which is generally a temporary state of affairs, anxiety is a state of being without any apparent source, and therefore, with no apparent beginning or end. Or better, its source or object is life itself. Anxiety, rampant,

---

5. There is a long history to discussions of American anxiety—from Patricia Mellancamp, *High Anxiety: Catastrophe, Scandal, Age and Comedy* (Bloomington: Indiana University Press, 1992), to Ruth Whippman, *America the Anxious* (New York: St. Martin's, 2016) and Plan C, "We are all very anxious" http://tinyurl.com/y9ywtzgm

universal and banal, incorporates everything. Rather than creating singular events or moments with such affective intensity that they explode through and thus remove themselves from the everyday affective landscape, anxiety makes everything into an emergency or crisis—the fact that anything might suddenly become a crisis already makes it so. Everything is a crisis waiting to jump out and take over one's being. Always experienced in the present, anxiety is yet always a futurity, operating in a future tense. It renders crisis banal, a new normal, a never-ending normalization of the state of emergency as it were. The sense of perpetual emergency becomes ordinary, everyday experience. But its banality or normalization does not mean that anxiety becomes comfortable, habitual, or even livable. It is rather like existing in a perpetual state of virtual "angst" (for lack of a better term) or disquiet about life itself. Rather than compassion fatigue, we might talk about risk fatigue, catastrophe fatigue, failure fatigue, victimage fatigue. Anxiety often goes hand and hand with depression since it defines a sense that one is unable to escape from, or gain control over, what appear to be the externally created, constantly anxiety-producing contours of one's life.[6]

This sense of anxiety is constantly being produced for us, in the smallest details of our lives and in our everyday discourses. One small example that I came across as I was writing this: a headline in the *New York Times* claims these are "boom times for new dystopians."[7] Really? It turns out that a boom is "several" novels that are "channeling the country's anxieties" with end-of-the-world narratives. They are no doubt expressing contemporary anxiety, and the forms in which they imagine the end of the world

---

6. One could add here a discussion of the changing affectivity of competition, where success or failure increasingly all comes down to the individual, and the ways they both induce and even require anxiety.

7. Alexandra Alter. "Boom times for the new dystopians," *New York Times*. March 30, 2017. https://www.nytimes.com/2017/03/30/books/boom-times-for-the-new-dystopians.html?_r=0

are no doubt related to contemporary figures of anxiety, but they are—and the *Times* is as well—producing that anxiety. Do they think that popular dystopian entertainment is new? That people have not imagined the end of the world? Really, where have they been for the past fifty years?

How does one respond to omnipresent anxiety? With a distracted hyperactivism, a constant sense of busy-ness and distraction. People commonly express the sense that everyday life seems to be colonized by endless tasks and endless demands on one's time. Everything feels more like either labor (how much time do I spend on the phone to accomplish some minor task that used to be done by some paid employee?), or a distraction (sometimes enjoyable, usually just annoying) from whatever it is—but I worry that I have lost it—that I had thought really mattered. Once again, understanding that we are all imbricated in this structure of anxiety may make visible a certain paradox inherent in the very attempt to defeat Trump, If Trump's success is constructed in part by ramping up anxiety, then opposing it might require us to stop constructing it as the coming end of the world, as evil, or stupidity or corruption incarnate. That is to say, the effort to defeat Trump, to some extent, may be yet another expression of the very affective structure of feeling that the new conservative assemblage is using to establish itself.[8]

The third structure of feeling, narcissism, involves the increasingly diminished scale of and investment in forms of

---

8. Ghassan Hage, *Against Paranoid Nationalism* (Annandale, NSW: Pluto Press, 2003) describes a particularly anxious—or in his terms—paranoid form of nationalism, in which one has to defend the nation against threats although, in some sense, one knows that it is not worth defending. How can "America" be both great and a catastrophe, simultaneously? You worry about the nation when you feel threatened but it is the structure of feeling of anxiety that makes everything into a threat, and makes all resources (e.g., jobs, wealth, mobility, the future) into a zero-sum game, thus ramping up the anxiety and the sense that the nation is always under attack from both the inside and the outside.

sociality, and a radical personalization of everything, which is redrawing the boundaries between public and private. This has resulted in a turning inward for the grounds of judgment and an increasing revelation of the self in public (e.g., confessional and reality TV, Facebook, etc.). Many commentators have blamed these developments on neoliberalism (which devalues the social and puts the burden on individual risk and responsibility), on the culture of consumption that has spoiled the millennials, and on the new media that have displaced personal relations into public domains. But I think these arguments have it backwards: these changes have contributed to the emergence of a new structure of narcissism that has, in turn, called such developments into existence. Of course, narcissism is not a new structure of feeling but there is something new about its current form. Unlike the narcissism of the 1970s (the "me-decade") which was largely defined by consumption, hedonism and self-gratification, and the narcissism of the '90s and early 2000s, which was largely defined by a sense of entitlement, today's narcissism is defined by an increasing sense of personal omnipotence that is amplified by its close connection to affective autonomy and hyperinflation on the one hand, and anxiety and hyperactivism on the other.

Consider what is likely to be a controversial example: mindfulness. "Mindfulness" has a long history as meditation, before it became a commodity and a cure for anxiety. Today, mindfulness suggests that the solution to one's personal anxieties, and even to the problems of the world, comes only from centering on oneself. Apparently, living completely in the present moment (an old hippie appropriation of an even older Buddhist idea) is supposed to be a defense against our anxieties and the pressures that produce them. We are told to turn our thoughts away from the past and the future (see the following discussion about temporal alienation), but I wonder if that does not mean away from the real political struggles that do and should demand our attention.[9] Some critics have argued that mindfulness is a luxury available only to those who have the time, but I wonder if it is not also a wonderfully paradoxical practice that, while calming your anxiety for the moment, is likely to only augment it in the long run. After all, mindfulness is yet another in a long line of demands for self-improvement. The answer to life's anxieties, complications and problems is in your hands. Be more mindful. Don't change the world, change yourself instead. And if and when you fail—because you will—the world and the problems it poses are not going away—then you are the problem. *You* have failed!

Contemporary narcissism may find its most telling expression in the transition from "the personal is political" to "the political is personal," giving rise to a new micro-politics that is completely individuated,[10] and produces an historically unique iteration of an affective appeal to the status of experience and feeling as the only true source of value and truth. And since the truth of experience is in some sense unassailable, the result is its sacralization, so that experience trumps knowledge or expertise, a point at which conservatives and fractions of the left come together. But the effects of this structure of feeling can be seen as well operating in federal laws on terrorism (e.g., the Animal Enterprise Terrorism Act), which defines violence and victimage entirely from the perspective of the offended party.

Perhaps the contemporary sanctification of markets (and the fact that people trust corporations over governments) and the all-too-easy return of forms of inequality and prejudice are themselves grounded in the primacy of personal experience. In the case of corporations, we interact with "corporate identities"

---

9. Contrary to the assumption that we need to slow down because the present is characterized by speed and acceleration, see Sarah Sharma, *In the Meantime* (Durham, NC: Duke University Press, 2014).

10. Whether this is subjectified or pre-individualized is a topic of theoretical debate.

and corporate businesses in the marketplace all the time in our everyday lives, and for the most part, these interactions are not only free of problems, but provide the necessary conditions of our lives. Somewhat paradoxically, corporations are up close and personal; they are on our shelves, in our pockets and homes, and on every screen we see. The knowledge and memory of corporate corruption, failure and mistreatment seems to be easily forgotten, especially since it rarely forms part of our personal experience (but is filtered through the media). And the least popular corporations—airlines, banks, etc.—are often those with which we have only occasional interactions but their impact, when we do, is immediate and personal. On the other hand, for the most part, the federal government remains distant from our experience, and most of its activities that impact our lives remain largely invisible; we have only rare interactions with its agents and, unfortunately, those interactions often feel impersonal, uncomfortable, understaffed and over-bureaucratized. Something similar, although ever more paradoxical, may partly explain the rising levels of racism and xenophobia. There is some evidence that such feelings are more likely in populations that live in segregated areas or areas far from the borders, where they do not actually have to encounter people of color or immigrants. If the radical re-segregation of residential space, which makes the experience of others less available, is partly responsible for the racial polarization of the country, then we are caught in a vicious circle.[11]

The irony is that this narcissism comes at the price of any sense of a relation between authenticity and character. In previous moments, being authentic meant putting one's character on display, being transparent or in some imagined sense, unmediated, in one's actions and statements. But contemporary narcissism has redrawn the line between public and private, so that, first, there is nothing that is necessarily private and second, there is nothing

---

11. I thank the Class working group for this insight.

that is not always and already mediated. And yet the very fact of universal mediation makes some things feel immediate and unmediated. Transparency and privacy are products of the forms of public-ness we adopt. Character becomes a matter of "personal branding," creating a sense of credibility as an image without content, in a kind of affective literalism: believe the image. It is, for example, Trump's image— that he "shoots from the hip" and tells it like it is—that constitutes his character and authenticity. It does not matter that his actions contradict his speech, and whatever is revealed about his character in his actions is apparently not relevant to his authenticity. His partisans are apparently not troubled by the glaring disparities. This is a new sense of what constitutes the relation of a person to his or her truth, and the relation of personal truth to the public domain.

The last structure of feeling I want to describe involves a historically specific form of alienation or anomie: a temporal alienation, a sense that time itself has become strange. The experience of it is well captured in the following quotation:

Amongst people who have utterly given up on the future, political movements don't need to promise any desirable and realistic change. If anything, they are more comforting and trustworthy if predicated on the notion that the future is beyond rescue, for that chimes more closely with people's private experiences … Brexit was never really articulated as a viable policy, and only ever as a destructive urge, which some no doubt now feel guilty for giving way to. Thatcher and Reagan rode to power by promising a brighter future, which never quite materialised other than for a minority with access to elite education and capital assets. The contemporary populist promise to make Britain or American "great again" is not made in the same way. It is not a pledge or a policy platform; it's not to be measured in terms of results … The Remain campaign continued to rely on forecasts, warnings and predictions, in the hope that eventually people would be dissuaded from "risking it." But to those that have given up on the future already, this is all just more political rhetoric. In any case, the entire practice of modelling the future in terms of "risk" has lost credibility, as evidenced by the now terminal decline of opinion polling as a tool for political control [at least, one might add, in some countries].[12]

The question of temporality is crucial to understanding the contemporary conjuncture, for it involves the pain of remembering the future and the enjoyment of forgetting (or at least rewriting) the past. This is one of the contradictions defining the conjuncture. What happens when a political economy/ideology based on an imagined future captures power, and yet, that future seems to recede into the past? The result might first seem to be a sense of the loss of control? But then the past has to be reconstructed: when did we have control? Over what? If the very imagination of control and agency assumes a stable imaginary, how can loss be constructed in relation to an unstable temporality? In fact, they have become the site of many different struggles at the level of the war of positions (e.g., around progress, youth, apocalyptic imaginaries, memory, etc.). Whatever the intentions of those engaging in such struggles, the very fact that time itself, the ways in which we organize, understand and live time, have been politicized and increasingly unstable and uncertain, points us to this structure of temporal alienation.

Perhaps common sense still tells us that time is the continuous unfolding of history, the relations of past (memory), present (experience) and future (anticipation) defined by the sliding of the present into the past and the future becoming present. But as the claim of progress has been deconstructed, as the predictability of the future and the knowability of the past have become less certain,

12. Will Davies, "Thoughts on the Sociology of Brexit," June 24, 2016. www.perc.org.uk/project_posts/thoughts-on-the-sociology-of-brexit/

one can only feel anxious about the responsibility of the present to the future, and the reliability of the past as a source for judgment of the present. Instead, one has images of time as apocalyptic (in its Christian, leftist and environmentalist forms), or of attempting to live with the radical uncertainty of the future. But perhaps the most common experience is that of being perpetually "stuck" in an inescapable immediacy. Being stuck is not just the absence of mobility but the very impossibility of mobility, or perhaps, in contemporary experience, the sense that mobility is running backwards. It is the absence of the temporality that is required for agency, and the only response appears to be the celebration of the very fact of survival, endurance, resilience, of the capacity to wait it out.[13] This commitment to the inevitability of staying the same, of staying in the same place, is itself temporally displaced since it is both an appeal to an imagined past (before mobility was possible) and the response to the failed future (when mobility would be absolute).

This is more than a change in the structures of time, and not merely an experience of being strangers in a strange time. It is not nostalgia for a never existed past,[14] nor for a future that failed to materialize. It is nostalgia for the very (im)possibility of a past and future, a melancholia in the future perfect (progressive) tense, leaving us stuck in a present that has stalled. (Incidentally, since "subjectivity" is intimately connected to the now of the present, this temporal alienation is itself intimately connected to the forms of narcissism and fanaticism—the sense of frustration, betrayal and rage—described above.) The result is, on the one hand, what is too easily described as a kind of general and popular amnesia of the past, a kind of active forgetfulness, which is often linked

13. See Ghassan Hage, "On stuckedness," in *Alter-Politics* (Melbourne: Melbourne University Press, 2015).
14. Every age seems to have its own imagination of some past golden age to which it hearkens back, but this is an ever-receding appeal.

to a spectacularization (as an expression of hyperinflation) of the trivial, the ordinary, the lie, and, on the other hand, the absence of any responsibility to the future. Both the past and the future have collapsed into a new sense of the anxious immediacy of the now. People are stuck in a present that does not feel real, i.e., that does not feel present. It is as if time itself were stuck. It is neither simply that both the past and the future have ceased to exist in the present, or that they exist only in the present. The crisis of our moment is not that the world is changing, nor that it is not changing; it is that the very notion of change itself is changing. It is not surprising that people feel—in all possible senses—out of time, a kind of melancholic echo.

This is an alienation in and from time: strangers in a strange temporality. It is an alienation of time itself, a time that is increasingly out-of-joint, out of place, out of time. This is an affective alienation from the temporality of one's own existence in time, as if, somehow, time itself has gone wrong. It is both nostalgia and hope for what can never be, for what could never have been. This sense of a-temporality—that there is something wrong with time itself, is not quite the same as the more postmodern sense of "the forever now," which assumes that all times have collapsed into or can be inscribed within the present; a-temporality is not merely the presence of many times, but the sense of an inability to differentiate time itself, the absence of a bounded present. We might even say that time itself has become chaotic.

This has implications for the ways we view time, the past as well as the future. The past has been both emptied and supersaturated; we remember everything and nothing simultaneously. We have subcontracted the past to the Internet, which returns it to us in ever unpredictable ways. To raise just one example: it has been the "norm" of the entertainment industries to retell history from a particular political perspective and even to exaggerate that perspective over all others; to use a cliché, history is (re)written by the victors or by those who control the means of communication and representation. Much of American popular culture, especially in post-war liberalism, celebrated "American exceptionalism"— war movies, westerns, etc. This was both critically predictable and retrospectively obvious. But it does feel like something else is going on. What happens to history in a culture dominated by affect instead of representation, by individuality and identification rather than politics? My favorite example: Hamilton, the most vociferous critic of democracy, affectively re-imagined in the popular through his biography, becomes a hero for the urban left. But this is perhaps one of the least offensive examples of recent rewritings—making up anew—of history. The very category of history is reconfigured, and history is being rewritten not from the perspective of the victor or even from some partisan perspective (although that still happens frequently enough), but by the determinations of affective economies, technological possibilities and creative profit-making. It is as if history had no reference back to the past as anything but a convenience and a contrivance, a cornucopia of opportunities for entertainment profits. In some sense, in the contemporary relation to history, the past itself becomes a chaotic collection of images and affects to be taken up and arranged at will and, as a result, the past is erased in the name of the hyperinflated affectivity of the present.

In relation to anxiety, this is experienced as what psychologists call "awfulizing," in which any event is immediately transformed into its worst-case scenario. As the future has been rendered irrelevant in and even unreal for the present, the result is a transformation of the possible temporalities of political struggle, for one does not act now to prevent what one knows is going to happen. One only acts after the fact, when it is, for all practical purposes, too late (e.g., global climate change or abortion rights), echoing what Benjamin might have called a left wing melancholia, a quietude that Hall once diagnosed as the left's growing anachronism. It is as if it is always too soon too late;[15] there is no present that can be the right time. And in fact, the very notion of politics as policy, as a response in the present directed toward the future back onto the present, become irrelevant if not impossible. I do not mean to ignore the obvious reality that there are political challenges, struggles, mobilizations and activisms continuing to happen, but I think that understanding such developments involves exploring the different ways in which they are inhabiting and deploying (or failing to do so) these emergent temporalities and alienations.

---

15. Meaghan Morris, *Too Soon Too Late* (Bloomington: Indiana University Press, 1998).

PART III

A Conjunctural Politics

7

Back to the Present: A Reactionary Counter-modernity

How do you tell a story, especially when you have too many possible characters and events, and no definitive plotline? I think of it as trying to construct one of those jumbo jigsaw puzzles— you know the kind I mean: 1,000 pieces and 900 of them are sky blue—when someone has dumped all the pieces from half a dozen puzzles and thrown away the pictures. I want to gather together the pieces—what we think we know about Trump and about the context, the war of positions, the complexity of conservatisms and the affective landscape—and try to assemble a story. I will offer one vision of what is going on, and where it might lead us. It is not the only story; Republicans could easily fall back into the project of the New Right, or even into global neoliberalism, but the one I propose is, I think, the most frightening, and so the one we should be sure does not come into being. It foreshadows the emergence of an unstable, hybrid political formation/project—not simply a neo-liberal (New Right) conservatism, or a reactionary conservatism, or a right-wing populism or a neo-fascist white supremacism. This reactionary counter-modernity is deeply involved in the emerging sense of political and cultural chaos. I will describe three dimensions of its possible political project: (1) the primacy of culture (and affect), (2) expressed in specific cultural forms and practices, (3) calling for the re-imagination of politics. Although I will write this in the past pluperfect (it has become), it is actually taking place in the future subjunctive (it may well happen).

It's All About the Culture

Culture has become the dominant level of social existence (over both politics and economics); it is culture that mediates—and even occasionally pre-empts—politics and economics, so that rather than thinking about political economy, we need to start by thinking about political cultures and the cultures of economy. This doesn't mean that capitalism is not still a powerfully determining force, but that, as I shall suggest toward the end of this chapter, it has become more a matter of corporate culture than of market relations. At the same time, without suggesting that the state no longer matters, politics has become largely affective; rather than a matter of ideologies or policies, it is all a matter of how one feels and the power or right to act upon such feelings. As Matt Taibbi suggested, Trump's victory makes the GOP a mood, not a party.[1] While previous New Right alliances offered ideological positions and struggled to change common sense, they neither sought nor won agreement, instead capturing popular consent built on affective appeals. But the balance has changed and with Trump, neither consent nor consensus defines the problematic of politics.

We need to rethink the way populism works, and differentiate between Trump's cultural populism (to whatever extent his appeal is populist), Sander's economic populism and Obama's political populism. My point is that the difference between Sanders and Trump was not merely that one had progressive and the other reactionary or chaotic politics, but that they were operating on different terrain. Both Sanders and Obama constructed a problem space in which an economic crisis is articulated to a social-

---

1. Matt Taibbi, *Insane Clown President* (New York: Spiegel & Grau, 2017).

democratic crisis (a surplus [or lack] of democracy) in the context of nationalist or globalist appeals. Trump's politics are cultural: the problem space is reconstructed so that matters of both economics (reduced largely to the lived immediacy of jobs and taxes) and democracy (the relations between majorities and minorities) are displaced into the relations of nationality and difference, and political polarization is translated into cultural polarization.

Populism is about ways of imagining and organizing the political field, usually but not necessarily based on some sort of egalitarian construction of "the people" against the elite. It is also a strategy or style of creating and organizing political constituencies, like "we the people." But populism can also be located in a different tradition—the popular, or what Bakhtin characterized as the "carnivalesque." Here populism is an antagonistic flaunting of the "low" or common styles of living, precisely as a refusal of the rules of civility and propriety, of the assumption that everything has its own proper place and form. The popular is vulgar, vernacular and polysemic; it is coarse, uninhibited and uncensored; it embraces bad manners. It is unmediated by the rules of civility, order and politeness. Interestingly, this cultural populism seems to have found its home in places that have traditionally been thought of as polite, civil, etc., at least within their own proscribed limits, such as the South and the Midwest. When this sense of the popular is brought in to redefine political struggle, the high/low distinction displaces or at least discomforts the left/right difference. This is the assemblage of Trump's support: innocent, ordinary people versus the elite snobs (with their rules and norms, their assumption that they are better than everyone else and therefore have the right to dictate how everyone should live—"properly"). Recently, those elite snobs have embraced so-called "subjugated minorities," who continue to live off the unearned, forced generosity of others, rather than showing any sympathy for the subordinated majority (the common folk), but who act improperly, uncivilly, and even vulgarly. Such cultural populism is almost always affective and often depends upon the personal authority and vitality of its leaders, even as the leader must present him- or herself as one of—just an arbitrarily chosen stand-in for—"the people."

The movement of politics onto the ground of culture has profound consequences for matters of identity. As identity is increasingly equated with culture, and culture with identity, it has become the touchstone for a new political apparatus, especially since culture here is itself increasingly defined affectively. The organization of society into identitarian categories that are correlated in specific ways to the organizations of power has a long, complex and changing history.[2] It defines the ways one inhabits and experiences ecologies of belonging and difference, even in the face of dispossession. They are neither unique to the U.S. in the twenty-first century, nor are they universal and invariable. On the contrary, they are articulated in different ways, embodied in different practices, and assigned to different populations, in different contexts.

Racism and colonialism have been constitutive of the U.S. since its founding, and have become so imbricated into the everyday life of the nation that some have described it as foundational to the American definition of the good life; this role was re-inscribed in post-war liberalism and its construction of the American dream. The Civil Rights movement in the 1950s challenged it by re-politicizing identity as the basis of legal and social inequality, and by "spiritualizing" and moralizing the material realities of such inequalities. While it was a multi-ethnic and multiracial opposition to racism, later forms of political struggle

---

2. For example, in the mid-twentieth century, identity became an important social issue in the face of questions about the difference between liberal democracy and forms of totalitarianism (communism and fascism). Identity was a way to think about the relationship between the individual and society. The terms of the discussion were set early on, in notions like an "identity crisis," as a task of individual authenticity against pre-assigned and pre-defined social roles.

were organized around the defense of particular identities. These movements equated opposition to forms of domination and oppression with the defense of the identities of the oppressed. Here identity was, simultaneously, collective and psychological—a tension held together by the concept of subjectivity, and defined by the problematics of visibility, access and recognition. As a result, such identity movements could not avoid assuming some measure of authenticity (essentialism) which was somehow constituted somewhere between the individual (body, experience) and the social (history, institutions).[3] Still, these movements were rarely "merely cultural," but focused as well on matters of redress and redistribution.

But increasingly, appeals to identity simultaneously created and set limits to collectives; it created a calculus of inclusion and exclusion, and defined an aspirational politics of possession or performance—as if one must possess the proper marker, perform the authentic display. Politics became an unmediated expression or statement of one's embodiment of the marker of communal equivalence. There could be no politics of representation except through authenticity. The only allowable politics flowed directly from the authenticity of one's experience of subordination, which is the direct result of one's identity. In other words, identity becomes an explanation of one's subordination rather than what needs to be explained. The result is, as Wendy Brown has argued, a politics of resentment in which one's position in the world is

---

3. Some critics, especially in the academy, have emphasized that the identities being defended are the product of the very regimes of power they are attempting to defeat, the end of a story about forms of liberal individuality rather than its beginning. They have argued that identities are all and always hybrid—never "pure" or homogeneous, or even intersectional, that they are always contextually constituted and hence, changing, and that the relationship between social categories of identity, subjectivity and agency is more complicated and contradictory than extant notions of identity allow.

seen only through a lens of being a victim.[4] And therefore, any others not similarly wounded are "privileged." The only way that someone not subject to that specific experience of subordination (and therefore not possessing that identity) can be "on the side of the victim" is to acknowledge their own privilege and complicity in victimizing the subordinated. One cannot renounce or overcome it because it is written into ... whatever mark of identity one does or does not have.

In the contemporary affective landscape, such notions of identity easily slide into a matter of individual feelings, erasing the complexity and structural realities of the relationship between politics and identity. But this notion of identity as culture, and culture as affect,[5] is easily appropriated as something that belongs to anyone who cares to embrace it—hence white identity and even white identity as victimage. It becomes a new fundamentalism and as such, it can serve as a powerful response to, and as a first line of defense against, the relativism, anxiety and alienation of everyday life. Consider for example what I would call "Christian pessimism": the perception that Christians or at least orthodox Christians (and to give Richard Dreher credit, he also includes orthodox Jews) have become outcasts and will soon be blacklisted in a "new Dark Ages."[6]

At the same time, the nation was becoming increasingly aware of its racist heritage and the continuing presence of racism, and difference itself became incorporated into the calculations of capitalism and the state. This complex situation meant that the

---

4. Wendy Brown, *States of Injury* (Princeton, NJ: Princeton University Press, 1995).

5. Think of the current fascination with and commodification of "ancestry," in which ancestry is first linked to DNA, which slides into place, which slides into culture and then into feelings. So because my DNA says part of me is from some place, I take up the culture and I feel who I am.

6. Richard Dreher, *The Benedict Option* (New York: Sentinel, 2017).

taken-for-granted practices, the older dominant forms, of what had become "normalized racism" failed. In a paradoxical way, racism was no longer doing its job.[7] In a difficult but ironic sense, we might say that racism was not in crisis; we have had a crisis of racism. But precisely because it is so intimately connected to our structures of feeling, and in particular to the hatred and violence of the culture of cruelty, the nature of the polarization that has defined U.S. political culture since the 1960s has changed as well. The new status of identity as culture offers a new legitimation for the increasingly visible and harsh punishment of those who violate the "culture," based on the transformation (not only of race as identity) but of racism itself. Of course, this does not mean that other racist histories, discourses and practices are not still operating, but I am trying to understand what is new or emergent.

But the culturalization of identity goes one step further in the project I am imagining: since race is so intimately connected with the nation, the re-invention of race and racism also signals the re-invention of the nation and a newly resurgent nationalism, a "white nationalism" in which both "whiteness" and the nation are defined in purely cultural terms, although actually, the terms of this national culture are never clearly defined. Here the complicated relations of race, ethnicity and nationality (which have led to the construction of such hybrid categories as "brown") are radically and even violently simplified: race = ethnicity = culture = nationhood. The notion of a nation here is in some ways an old one. It is not Huntington's civilizational understanding precisely because it is nationalist. But it is also a new, fanatical (in the sense defined above) rejection of the very possibility of multiculturalism, in what is now offered as a "post-racist" regime.

In this national formation, anyone can be white, anyone can be "American." But it is also the case that anyone can be other, can be outside the nation. The nation is symbolically raced and ethicized,

---

7. This is, I think, the condition that gives rise to Afro-pessimism.

but those identifications are affective. Its politics are mediated only by the affectivity of identity that assumes—insists on—a cultural, affective homogeneity. Such an equivalence legitimates all sorts of violence and coercion. In a miracle of circular logic, it legitimates one to feel like the victim even as one attacks and victimizes the other as an outsider, and it legitimates the attack precisely because he or she has victimized you.[8] For example, in this reconstituted nation, terrorism is always an act done on the nation as a culture so that, by definition, a terrorist cannot be a part of the nation, cannot be "American." (Think of the ways home-grown terrorists are described as "born in America," suggesting that they are not really American.) When an other acts against the nation, all considerations of causes, of personal or social history, or of intentions become irrelevant, while acts of violence perpetrated by "Americans" are always something to be explained (away)—by external forces or severe mental problems.[9] The link between identity, culture, nation and victimage is perhaps partly what explains the legitimation of the presence of neo-reactionary white nationalists in the Trump administration but also Trump's consistent refusal to renounce acts of hatred and violence in anything but the most subdued terms, unless they are enacted upon the "American" nation.

But this cultural nationalism leaves unanswered the obvious question: what is the content of "American" culture? It is not the sense of an "American creed" that was put forth by conservatives in the 1980s and '90s. Thus it is not quite the sense of the modern nation, a people united around a shared set of norms and a shared narrative. It is not exactly about ideology and consensus, although it certainly has to do with a sense of individuality and freedom, but there must be something more, something that remains, for the moment undefined. I shall return to it shortly.

8. See Lundberg, "Enjoying God's death."
9. I am grateful to Kumi Silva for this insight.

It's All About the Chaos

The second observation I want to make about this emergent project is that it is highly dependent on the forms of mediation made available in contemporary media, including forms of immediacy and dis-intermediation, personalization, affectivity and, perhaps most importantly, the production of a kind of baroque chaos. Many of these discursive practices depend upon changes in technological capacities, and upon Trump's deeply ambivalent relation to various media.

Most of the discussions of the role of the media in the election have noted the differences in the ways the two candidates related to them. Clinton used big data with the logics of demographics, while the Trump campaign apparently put its resources into social media, putting big data in the service of micro-targeted marketing (tailored messages, the manipulation of sentiment, self-learning algorithms) to personalize, for example, Facebook ads.[10] The right has generally been more adept at using the possibilities of digital media, multiplying its presence to occupy more and more space, manipulating Google's PageRank system, using (if not creating) various trolling practices—upsetting and humiliating its opponents, gaining attention, inciting micro-panics, creating chaos. Clinton relied on celebrity endorsements, as if these still defined the currency of political campaigns. Trump, on the other hand, played the traditional media for all they are worth, gaining free—unmediated—access to his audiences (since his speeches and rallies were often broadcast live and unedited) and therefore, was largely able to set the public agenda.

---

10.   See Carole Cadwalladr, "Cambridge Analytica affair raises questions vital to our democracy." *Guardian.* https://www.theguardian.com/politics/2017/mar/04/cambridge-analytica-democracy-digital-age, and Cathy O'Neill, *Weapons of Math Destruction* (New York: Crown, 2016).

As soon as one begins to talk about Trump and media, one has to face the elephant in the room: the matter of Trump's lies, fake news, alternative facts, and post-truth, which has turned out to be one of those occasions when the left's only response seems to be either panic, or a naïve and dangerously a-historical and elitist appeal to the idea that "the truth, compellingly told, is enough."[11] (At the very least, we might want to imagine new forms of judgment, new forms of comparison, new forms of authority and trust, in an age of fanaticism and polarization.) But I do not want to spend too much time on this because it is one of those struggles which, given the context, can't be won, since "truth" has always been in crisis as it were. So let me limit myself to a few observations.[12]

That governments (and presidents) lie is not new(s). The United States has a long history of political lying. During Bush's administration, Colbert introduced the notion of "truthiness." And Karl Rove made his infamous statement:

> The aide said that guys like me were "in what we call the reality-based community," which he defined as people who "believe that solutions emerge from your judicious study of discernible reality." ... "That's not the way the world really works anymore," he continued. "We're an empire now, and when we act, we create our own reality. And while you're studying that reality—judiciously, as you will—we'll act again, creating other new realities, which you can study too, and that's how things will

11. Mark Hertsgaard, "Progressives Need to Build Their Own Media," *The Nation*, March 20, 2017. https://www.thenation.com/article/progressives-need-to-build-their-own-media/

12. Some of the following discussion draws from ongoing research by the COMM 750 Media Group and was presented by Xuenan Cao, Sherah Faulkner and Lucas Power in a class project "What's so funny about truth, post-truth, and Trump gibberish?".

sort out. We're history's actors ... and you, all of you, will be left to just study what we do."[13]

But we can go back much further. My favorite story is that several of the "founding fathers," using pseudonyms, published opinion pieces in the press filled with lies about their opponents and/ or their positions. Then they published another piece, under a different pseudonym, praising the original lies. Fake news?

That the media lie is not new(s). William Buckley began the *National Review* in 1955 to counter the biases of the establishment media. The left Movement of the 1960s constantly accused the mainstream media of lying—about the war, about protests, etc. And it has continued to protest the lies of the media ever since. This may be in part the result of the particular contradictions of media economies—in which the news ("facts") are commodities that are expensive to produce and yet over which the media have little control.

There has never been "objective" news. The idea is a relatively recent one; most news has always been biased. In fact, the history of journalism and media is replete with crises and debates about the nature of truth and its relation to democracy.[14] As historian Michael Schudson put it, objectivity "seems to have been destined

---

13. Ron Suskind, "Faith, Certainty and the Presidency of George W. Bush," *New York Times Magazine*, October 17, 2004. www.nytimes.com/2004/10/17/magazine/faith-certainty-and-the-presidency-of-george-w-bush.html?_r=o

14. The first effort at "objective" news was the so-called "penny press," which opposed itself to the more elite partisan press in the name of a popular egalitarianism (Jacksonianism), and opened the door to (often rather objectionable) advertising. Here "objectivity" meant neutrality, although it often included false stories (called "humbugs"). The problem of objectivity was revisited in the Newspaper Publicity Act of 1912, and again in the 1920s, in the defense of an objectivity linked to professionalization, and again in the 1947 Hutchins Commission Report, which advocated a social responsibility approach over free market libertarianism.

to be as much a scapegoat as a belief, more an awkward defense than a forthright affirmation."[15] We might be better off seeing the contemporary question of fake news and alternative facts as signaling yet another crisis of democracy and "the free press."

The difference between bias and lies is itself an historical construct and the line varies with the context. One can say that there is a difference between honest mistakes, bias and the intentional lies of Fox, Trump and Breitbart, but that already assumes what one must prove.

The idea of an objective Truth has been deconstructed by many of the same groups on the left, including scholars from philosophers to sociologists, that now want to come to its rescue. Knowledge and truth (even scientific truth), it turns out, are constructions, the product of relations among institutions—of research and education (including, in the case of news, journalism schools), governments and corporations. "Facts" are simply those statements we think cannot be denied. Varieties of social constructionism, especially those which emphasized the necessarily political and perspectival nature of knowledge, have tilted the academic debates, without ever having bothered to mount compelling arguments, especially in public, of why this need not lead us into relativism.[16] While the New Right attacked constructionism and relativism, the new reactionary assemblage seems to have embraced it. Trump is merely social constructionism gone mad, in public, with great relish. It is social constructionism as the new fundamentalism. It is all made worse by the fact that those very institutions that supposedly recognize and carry the truth to the people have failed far too often, at least in the eyes of many people—too

15. Michael Schudson, *Origins of the History of Objectivity in the Professions: Studies in the History of American Journalism and American Law 1830–1940* (New York: Garland, 1990), p. 269.
16. Even Plato, the arch-enemy of relativism, recognized that "we see with our minds not our eyes."

many contradictions, too many corrections, too many unnecessary panics (remember Y2K?).

The problem will not be solved by the creation of a left-wing media network. Still, there are questions that one might think to answer first. Why has this not succeeded before? How does one fund it? How does it operate given the new economy of the news, where what was once an unprofitable but high-status public service was brought under the discipline of the entertainment division, and expected to make—significant—profit.[17] What is its purpose: to mobilize one's base, to expand one's support, to unify the passionately dissenting fractions of the anti-Trump populace? Do we understand how Fox News, etc. was able to gather its audience and then construct its influence? Why do we focus so entirely on national media and largely ignore the role of local news (which is generally more widely trusted), which is increasingly owned by national (and often right-wing) companies, such as the Sinclair Media Group? Do we know how to create popular communication, especially in the form of "news"? Many on the left have never trusted pleasure, entertainment and popular culture to begin with; now they complain that they cannot speak effectively into the spaces of the popular.[18]

The power of fake news is one of desire. It is propaganda that is speaking to its acolytes rather than to the enemy. It is demand-side propaganda! It cannot be explained away as the result of the industrialization of news and propaganda (in a new entertainment-politics complex), although it is monetized propaganda.

Trump's lies and the many appeals of and to fake news are more frequent, more visible, more actively and intensely defended, even in the face of glaring counter-evidence. One has to assume that Trump

---

17. This change from a public service to a profit-making endeavor has affected all the news media, including print.

18. The exception is political comedy and satire, which often humiliates the opponent, but at its best, deconstructs the acts and claims of power.

(or someone in his staff) knows that they will be called out, and yet, they are confident that this will have no consequence other than multiplying and intensifying the chaos.

So what is going on? I think one has to look, not at the intention but the effects, and locate these practices within the new technological possibilities of the Internet, which has, at the very least, re-inflected the ambiguity of a relationship to reality—as truth and authenticity. Social media present "real events from real people in real time," embodying an "authenticity" that while unchallengeable is not necessarily true. But this is not merely a technological causality, for matters of what is real have always depended on matters of aesthetics and ethos. And these are inseparable from the political and affective landscapes I have described. Truth itself is becoming a matter of affect! The problem with fake news is not simply that it denies Truth, or even that it denies the possibility of judgment, but that it denies the necessity of judgment, the link between judgment and credibility. Without such a relation, one can no longer distinguish between trolling and bold speech (truth-telling as parrhesia).

Why? What is the purpose or better, what is the effect of this re-formation of the field of truth, authority and credibility? What is being produced is a field of discursive and epistemological chaos, in which statements and contradictions endlessly multiply and change. Statements, whether truths or lies, begin to take on a strange, almost eerie quality, as if they have a kind of autonomy and singularity, as if they were free-floating, not connected to anything. One can assume this is an accident, or that it is the unintended consequence of incompetence, but I think we have made that mistake too often, and we would do better to assume that there is a purpose behind the madness. Chaos indeed!

In fact, chaos seems to be a common theme in the cultural practices of this emergent reactionary counter-modernity. The new media are fragmenting, dispersing and integrating, constructing a kind of baroque assemblage in which an overwhelming sense of chaos is likely to be the most immediate response. For all the left's denunciation of Breitbart.com as content, there has been little discussion of what the website itself is doing, given that its appearance is entirely chaotic and in any tradition terms, almost impossible to read (extraordinarily cluttered with no apparent organization), and as much a store and a collection of advertisements as a source for news or political opinion. And, as I have already alluded, trolling is as much about the production of chaos as the politics of humiliation. This new politics of trolling is driven not only by a politics of affect and humiliation, but increasingly by the affective politics of fundamentalism, victimage, violence and hyperinflation. It is a narcissism of anonymity, a hyperinflation of anxiety, with no sense of a temporality that is anything other than the immediacy of a present with no substance of its own. If this is the new figure of politics, it is a politics without an ethics (which could be juxtaposed to the increasing propensity on the Left to offer an ethics without a politics). But trolling is also about producing an overwhelming sense of unpredictability, uncertainty and chaos.

Images and words, tiles and fragments, ads and merchandise, politics and editorial statements appear to be haphazardly thrown together (again, look at Breitbart.com). Is Breitbart.com, is Trump, trying to milk politics for retail purposes? Is Trump really the president so he can make money (selling hats? really?) or build his brand?[19] Or are they deconstructing the boundaries between economics and politics, not because it's all about the economy, but, as I will suggest, to tear down politics itself. One can see this intentional chaos in the very form of Trump's (and his administration's) communication: juxtaposing claims, phrases, thoughts and promises with little or no discernible relation, constantly contradicting oneself and each other. This is a mode of communication—rhetoricians call it "parataxis"—that is perfectly

---

19. Perhaps like Silvio Berlusconi.

congruent with the new attention economy. As Hebdige puts it, "The combination of vitriolic abuse, unsubstantiated assertion and extreme brevity—the short, shocking statement—this is the signature DNA of the successful tweet,"[20] and I might add, of trolling. While some argue (correctly I think) that this further severs the link between language and thought, it is more important to observe that it absolutizes the link between language and affect. In this new media culture, it is not just that one has a right to create whatever one wants, it's that (in postmodern terms), the difference between the various creations is, in a sense, indiscernible and incapable of being judged in anything but the old discarded terms. This is the hyperinflation of the assumptions that humans make their own reality, the *reductio ad absurdum* of the modernist hubris.

Moreover, this chaos is partly produced by taking up the affordances of these technologies. It is commonly observed that new media are all about the attraction, manipulation, capture, measurement and monetization of attention. Now, while the ability to do such things may have developed enormously in the past decade or two, this is not a new definition of how the media work. Dallas Smythe argued over fifty years ago that what the media were selling to advertisers was attention (eyes, I think he put it).[21] There are significant differences of course. The older attention economy was predicated on a sharp distinction between content (almost always defined as coherent if interrupted narratives), information (such as news) and advertising. The new attention economy does not make such sharp distinctions (driven in part by both technological and economic imaginaries, and enabled

20.   Dick Hebdige. "Un-presidented [*sic*]." Lecture presented at the University of California-Santa Barbara's Democracy Day, January 18, 2017.
21.   Dallas Smythe, "Communications: Blindspot of Western Marxism," *Canadian Journal of Political and Social Theory*, 1(3) (Fall 1977): 1–27.

by advancements in cognitive science put into the service of marketing strategists and media designers). Rather, messages can be radically subdivided, fragmented and reassembled (or not) into all sorts of strange hybridities, in ways that seem to amplify both affective autonomy, affect freed from the constraints of semantic meaning and conscious self-reflection, and temporal alienation.

Even as this affective attention economy tends to make everything equivalent, it also makes everything special, it makes everything into a spectacle, not just on the grand scale of staged events but also at the micro-level of images and statements. Everything becomes a performance, and the current use of sharp, shocking, in-your-face statements, visual and sonorial bites as it were, is no doubt part of its operation. And at the same time, it creates a sensation of unmediated experience. While this may be in part an illusion—our theories often tell us it must be— there is a kind of material and affective immediacy that allows, e.g., Trump's appeal to feel unfiltered, authentic and physically palpable. The result is less a matter of networking than of a hyper-personalization of constructionism that enshrines and normalizes narcissism.

The media have always reconfigured the relations of private and public spaces and experiences, as well as the relations of local, regional and national geographies of identities, but the new media have enabled the separation of community from any necessary anchor in either time or space (a post-geographical, post-historical form of collectivity or the social bond). And as they have removed communities from space, they have placed individuals in hyper-local places, and removed them from time (creating new figurations and imaginations of immortality).[22]

---

22. I do not mean to ignore the range of effects of the new information technologies of "big data" including forms of surveillance as well as complex forms of political, social and cultural profiling and targeting, linking money, networks, knowledge and "tastes."

In the new affective media, everyone is/can be a star; everyone's lives can and even should be documented, but the story does not end there, because the autonomy of affect is also a refusal of egalitarianism! As a result, documentation becomes a competition in which no one (thanks to hyperinflation) can accept just being average or normal. The new normal is to exceed. Extreme sports is the performance of social media in life. Everyone has to be, or appear to be, or make themselves be—all of which are the same thing now—the best. Is this an unearned entitlement or is it perhaps a new form of individuation? And in this competition, negative affects—suffering, pain, anger, rage—are easier to document and easier to inflate. They are increasingly the ways in which one constructs oneself as mattering.[23]

This is the landscape of the emergence of new political possibilities. The very figure of Trump stands in as a performer who affirms his power to construct truth affectively, not only to gain attention (because attention does matter) but to narcissistically affirm his heroic power and authority, in the truth of his fundamentalism and victimage against those who belittle him. That is the point: what he says is reality (it does not matter if what he says corresponds to any other reality) that creates a bubble into which others can choose, be invited or seduced to enter (not unlike, I might add, the way music functioned in the 1960s Movement). The result is that politics is brought completely into the realm of the popular (a move that has been happening since the 1960s). Entertainment is not merely a distraction or amusement but the field in which figurations and apparatuses of power compete to establish themselves, the field in which power claims fealty. The relation of politics and enjoyment has been so strongly cemented that is almost impossible to imagine how they can be separated.

---

23. This would seem to have serious implications not only for the nature of contemporary celebrity, but also for the role of celebrity in political culture.

Entertainment seems to have become both the storm and the shelter from the storm. It embodies the very affective landscape of our contemporary lives even as it produces it, and produces the impossible imagination of its escape. Hence Trump can claim, without protest, that he has had the highest rating since 9/11, and one of his Wall Street advisors (Alex Jones), whom Trump has cited frequently, can announce that he is "really" a performance artist. And if we are to combat Trump and the forces he has unleashed, we must find ways of entering into and rearticulating the popular, of locating and inflecting residual and emergent conditions of possibility that open up alternative pathways.

It's All About the Nation

The third and final observation I want to make about an emergent reactionary counter-modernity involves the vision of what one might call a new political order.[24] Trump's victory is sometimes read as the end of party politics, the end of democracy, the end of the rule of law. It may well be all those things but its possibilities only come into view if we contextualize these claims, and begin to think of what is being put in the place of "politics as usual," in fact, of politics as it has been thought of for quite some time, to think about the possibility of a new practice of governmentality. Foucault identified four such diagrams of governmentality,

---

24. One can imagine—or actually see—other directions in which some of these forces could refigure the modern liberal state. Meaghan Morris has pointed to Singapore as exhibiting many—but not all—of the features I am describing. See Chua Beng Huat, *Elections as Popular Culture* (London: Routledge, 2007), and *Liberalism Disavowed* (Ithaca, NY: Cornell University Press, 2017). In Singapore, and perhaps even contemporary China, Confucianism provides common cultural ground for normative and even decent behavior. In fact, I am told that Nick Land himself has moved to Shanghai and expressed admiration for Singapore and for the Confucianist approach to governmentality.

which he thought emerged over time but could and did co-exist. Power has operated as the power to kill, the power to surveil and discipline, the power to let live, and the power to define and locate risk; each is defined by its own form of rationality: sovereignty, individuation, probability and markets respectively. To elaborate just a bit: sovereignty operates through the singular presence of the monarch, discipline through surveillance of the individual body, biopower through the demographic division of the population and statistical probabilities to control their distribution and movements and finally, rather weakly in my opinion, neoliberalism through the designation of the market as the definition of state rationality and the construction of the entrepreneurial subject as the site of capital accumulation, investment and risk. I do not think any of these, including neoliberalism,[25] describes the significance of Trump's victory or of the project I am trying to foreshadow.

There are some who would locate this new order, the new diagram of governance, in the emergence of a new ontological power (pre-emption, for example) or at the feet of the new media technologies, an algorithmic society of control in which algorithms are assumed to have the literal power to control behavior through systems of decisions and commands.[26] I do not know if such claims are true, but they sound too much like the latest forms of decontextualized technological determinism, in this case, one

---

25. I'm not convinced that neoliberalism was ever a particularly useful description of where we have been for the past few decades.

26. Such a system does not deny the continuing relevance of the previous ones, but only insofar as they may define algorithmic sequences. Algorithms can use any of their logics, but again, need not because they can take advantage of others' procedural logics (decision trees, weighted differentials, etc.). They are neither probabilistic (clustering groups across time and space) nor stochastic (non-predictive) but procedural. Algorithms do not create populations or individuals; they aggregate and command sets of actions to produce singular outcomes.

that has finally arrived at the dream of behaviorism: the ability to determine outcomes. But they all too often simply repeat the long historical battle between utopian and dystopian narratives that have greeted every new technology. And they do not capture anything of the specificity of what is going on. That is, one must still ask the more contextual question of how such logics operate given the historical and affective contexts.

Trump's chaotic assemblage of conservatism points us in a different direction: the possibility of the emergence of an anti-political "alt-fascism," a reactionary, pre-modern (or is it postmodern?) vision of a nation without a state and an abso-lutization of culture without difference, thus clearing the space for the dispersed power of a new "popular corporatocracy." This reconfiguration of power begins by doing two things: first, it reconstructs the affective landscape as chaos, providing a context within which the project appears to become sensible and even normal. That entails a constant effort to disrupt what has been taken as the normal, everyday practice of politics, to deny the expected consequences of any action, and to refuse the expected response to any problem. What appears to be the condition of living in a state of continuous warfare, and a multiplication, perpetuation and even normalization of crises, creates chaos as the new bottom line. Unpredictability, what Arendt called a "system of systemlessness," is the goal. Despite what so many commentators claim, Trump is not causing the chaos. The chaos is what makes Trump effective. It is a grand refusal to organize, to be consistent, to follow through; the result is that nothing that happens seems to make sense. It is a crisis not of leadership but of organization, which then allows for the seeming failure of the existing organization of politics and opens the need to invent some other form of governance. This construction of chaos is a refusal to construct an organic crisis. In its place, the multiplicity and multiplication of crises flourishes, without any effort of unity, hyperinflating the anxiety that is already a fundamental feature of the affective landscape. And the only "reasonable" response is the demand for visible and immediate activity, almost as if any action, any change, is good. The response to the threat of complacency is hyperactivism, a disarticulated and disorganized assemblage of crises. The current political conjuncture is not merely one of fanaticism but of a chaotic hyperactivism. Or perhaps the new organic crisis is predicated not on fear as much as anxiety, in the face of an increasingly experienced chaos and the knowledge that the impending catastrophe could come from anywhere and take any shape.

Second, it must convince people that the democratic State—understood as a nation-state, as a unity of two functions or modes of operation—coercion and the production of publics and public goods—does not work and that their participation does not, cannot, and should not matter. The various New Right alliances over the past forty years have been consistently struggling to make representative democracy irrelevant if not impossible, both in perception and reality. Twenty-five years ago, I argued that the growing cynicism about and disinvestment from state politics and voting could only be understood if it were, in fact, part of a larger strategy. It seems that the very people we elect have acted to poison the integrity of elections, increasing the perception of their links to both money and partisan interests. Whether through rampant lobbying, secret and unlimited private and corporate campaign financing, increasing technocracy, polarization, gerrymandering (either silently but obviously aimed at racial and ethnic voters, or explicitly aimed at the opposition party), or voter suppression laws, it is not surprising that most people think that democratic partic-ipation in the state, and that even the democratic state itself, has failed. Most Americans believe that elections are unfair, dishonest and even rigged. Most believe that their vote, if they bothered to vote, does not matter. Most Americans believe politicians are—and presumably by extension, politics itself is—dishonest and dysfunctional. It is but a small step to argue that the fault is in the very idea of democracy and the form of the administrative state rather than in the failed efforts to achieve these goals.

Is it accidental that the president of the American Enterprise Institute advises people to "just let go of politics" since "The people most in the know [about politics] tend to be unhappier than those who pay less attention?" Basically, he suggests, since we feel like a "victim of political circumstances," we should abandon politics.[27] Democracy was supposed to give people some sense of control over their own and the nation's destiny. It has clearly failed. The modern nation-state was meant to solve the problems facing "the people," and it too has clearly failed. Is it any surprise that the result is either apathy or fundamentalism, or what Balibar calls post-political hegemony? The general problem of our time, he suggests, is constitutional: "a brutal oscillation between the seeming irreversible process of de-democratization and the possibility of a 'democratization of democracy' itself."[28] Although I know to what the latter phrase is referring, I think Balibar like many others is overly optimistic about the actual strategic effectiveness of such calls for radical democracy, especially in the contemporary context. Such anti-statist, horizontal politics often descries the failure of progressive state politics, but fails to examine the long history of failure that defines the history of such prefigurative efforts, including the Movement of the 1960s. Any oppositional struggle has to recognize that, under conditions of de-democratization, the state is no longer supposed to protect the minority from the majority but rather, to protect the rights of what thinks of itself as a majority (but is rapidly becoming a minority) precisely because it has defined the nation in cultural terms, to rule over the diversity constitutive of the (coming) majority. The

27. Arthur C. Brooks, "Depressed by politics," *New York Times*, March 18, 2017, p. A19.
28. Etienne Balibar, "'Populism' and 'counter-populism' in the Atlantic mirror." http://tinyurl.com/y7498ycm

problem is that, when both sides have constructed themselves in terms of identity and culture, and see themselves as victims, there is no space for mutual consideration or any notion of a deliberative community. Opposition becomes something bad for the nation.

This contempt for mutual consideration is more than just a restatement of the refusal of compromise. It is the rejection of politics itself as struggle and of ideology/policy as the stage on which political struggle is waged. It marks a growing sense that there cannot be meaningful policy disputes[29] precisely because one's position is always invested with the certainty of fundamentalism. What I know to be the solution to any problem seems so commonsensical that the fact that politicians cannot see it or choose to ignore it (either option basically defines politics) means that politics itself is corruption, selfishness and undeserved privilege. Of course, politics, ideology and partisanship always belong only to the other side, not to mine. But because I am a victim of politics, of government, the only solution is to reject them both entirely, and to find something new—not a new political position or solution but an outsider who can bypass politics all together but who is part of the nation-as-culture and so will, inevitably it seems, share the obviousness of the solution. Such a vision is only possible in part because of an assumption of the nation as a shared culture whose homogeneity is always predefined, which requires a fanatical rejection not of difference per se but of difference within the nation.

The nation-as-culture is the nation without the need of a state.[30] When Steve Bannon talks about "deconstructing the administra-

---

29.   See John Hibbing and Elizabeth Theiss-Morse, *Stealth Democracy* (Cambridge: Cambridge University Press, 2002).

30.   In a sense, this is the mirror image of Michael Hardt and Antonio Negri's vision in *Empire* (Cambridge, MA: Harvard University Press, 2001) as a de-centered global state without a nation. One might also think of Pierre Clastres's *Society Against the State* (New York: Zone Books, 1989) on societies that work actively against the possibility of a state formation, but one cannot simply substitute nation for society here.

tive state," it is easy and comforting to say that he is just another anti-regulation, anti-big government conservative, but that seems far off the mark. The administrative state is the modern state insofar as it is concerned with the production and protection of public life. Bannon is suggesting that we tear down politics as it is constituted as and by the sovereignty of the nation-state. How does one go about dismantling the politics of the state? You literally dismantle it, take it apart and get rid of as many pieces and as many functions as you can, even if people think that those functions (like protecting people from various sorts of bad things) might be good.

Such a project rejects the state as a civil bureaucracy—what Trump derides as the deep state that opposes him (certainly not what Peter Scott meant by the term). We need to take Trump's metaphor of "draining the swamp" seriously, if not literally. Draining the swamp is not the same thing as clearing away the garbage, and it does not mean merely squeezing or shrinking the state. Draining the swamp means transforming the ground itself, destroying whatever was standing on it, as the condition of possibility for building something entirely different on the land, something that could not have been imagined before the swamp was drained. It is the ultimate image of creative destruction— destruction comes before creation. This is Bannon's project: "to bring everything down." Perhaps it is not surprising that the desire to rewrite the Constitution has resurfaced with a new vitality and popular appeal—to re-make the very conditions of possibility of politics. What might this be: a return to the Articles of Confederation, giving power and autonomy back to the individuated states? Or would it go even further, dismantling the apparatuses of state power even at more local levels?

But in a way, this vision of a nation without a state simply carries to its logical conclusion a program that was hidden in plain sight (but never totally embraced) within the New Right—a vision of cutting taxes so much that the state could afford nothing but the military. But something more is operating. For this is not just the rejection of the political establishment and of established politics but a challenge to the very concept of government and governance—as representative democracy, as ideological and as capable of producing an ordered reality. Trump has unleashed the possibility of taking power while breaking the very system/ organization that is itself the expression and the agent of that power. Reactionary counter-modernity wants to occupy the state while dismantling it, and deconstructing politics.

It values culture over economics, and nationalism over globalism (read global capitalism), and often sees this as the only alternative (and an uncertain one at that) to the coming Racial Holy War, which, it is likely to claim, is the inevitable result of democracy and multiculturalism and not of its own racisms. So, it is vital that Fox News, Breitbart.com and friends constantly present the world as a dark and dangerous place, and the future as always on the edge of catastrophe, transforming anxiety into fear, to produce a sense of perpetual threat to the nation. And further, they must present this as new![31]

The challenge facing this imagined counter-modernity— its organic crisis as it were—is what is left after you dismantle "modern" politics? Here we must go back to the New Right, which imagined a state disarticulated from the nation, a state whose sole function is security and coercion, to defend the nation and its borders, leaving the nation itself as an isolated, social narcissist.[32]

---

31. This practice of constructing a sense of fear and threat, of society as constantly dangerous, has been a key aspect of post-war American culture (including politics, news, popular media and advertising), and a key element of the right's attempt to install a "law and order" platform, since the 1960s. This was a key empirical corollary of George Gerbner's "cultivation theory" and the "cultural indicators project," which he called the "mean world syndrome."

32. I am deeply grateful to Chris Lundberg for his help in thinking about these questions.

This state—encompassing the few institutions that remain largely trusted and respected (by a majority of the population at least) including the police and military and intelligence agencies— is no longer the modern state (and for at least part of the New Right, what must be coerced is a culture understood in specific moral terms).

But reactionary counter-modernity takes this one step further, beyond the imagination of a minimalist state defined as pure coercive force, for this "state" now stands in the place of the imagined unity of the nation, which is in need of constant protection. But what is it exactly that is in need of protection, that is under constant threat? Or to put it in the terms I used earlier, what defines the common culture that is the nation, what binds it together? This is where the future might get really scary.

Lots of people have described Trump and the forces he has released as fascist or at least, as the coming of fascism. The problem is that they have a single, fixed, decontextualized image of fascism—whether from Spain, Italy, or Germany. Furthermore, all too often we assume that fascism is a form of totalitarianism that embodies particular affective and ideological strategies[33] in order to make the state omnipresent and omnipotent. Contrarily, classic European fascism is perhaps better understood as a particular reconstruction of political economy, of the relationship between the state and corporations.[34] If "every age has its own proper fascism," then I am suggesting that our fascism, if that is what it is, is defined by its reconfiguration of the nation and the state: not merely by the minimization of the state to a necessary apparatus of surveillance, coercion and defense, but its reconstitution of a new kind of political economy, one without politics or a state as we understand it, one that has reduced the nation to an

---

33. See Umberto Eco, "Ur-Fascism." *New York Review of Books*, June 22, 1995. www.nybooks.com/articles/1995/06/22/ur-fascism/

34. This was in fact the conclusion of the Frankfurt School. I am grateful to Andrew Davis for all his help on these matters.

affective landscape of identity, and then identifies both with the single figure of the corporation.

That is, without meaning to sound paranoid (but even paranoids are right sometimes, if only in the future perfect tense), what is left to the nation is the evolving power of the corporation and corporate culture. The functions of the state in relation to the nation as publics, which have been deconstructed, are now ceded to the corporation. What is in need of protection—what defines the "white" nation is corporate culture, which extends far beyond the corporate form itself into the interstices of our everyday and institutional lives. But the corporation as an institutionalized cultural form no longer needs the state to protect it, only to give it legitimacy after the fact. It is the corporation that, at least in this imagined future, takes on the second operation of the state as well—security, coercion (through all sorts of forms of power) and defense. The corporation becomes the nation and the state, or perhaps, a nation without a state—a corporate society in which the difference between the pre-modern and the postmodern no longer matters.

That is, ironically, it is all about the economy but the economy is now understood as culture. It is no longer the state that creates and validates the existence of corporations but corporations that define and sanction the reality of states. It is not that the state is to be run as a corporation, or even that its various apparatuses are to be corporatized or privatized. The state is displaced into the service of an imagined "popular and dispersed corporatoc-racy," setting up a new fundamental contradiction: between the nation as culture and the economy as global. The symbol of this new corporatocracy is that of global corporations that can still be "branded" as American. (The most commonly invoked examples are primarily information and technology corporations.)[35]

---

35. This raises complicated questions about the spatiality of corporations and their insertion into national spaces. Some corporations—primarily technology corporations whose products address personal and public

In this alt-fascist model of governance, power is dispersed through and embodied quite literally in corporations, precisely as embodiments of a culture that increasingly defines the national culture even as it is articulated across spatial borders. The power of corporations is mediated through their deployment of culture as identity, especially in the convergence of technology, entertainment and security. The corporation is the perfect site of mediation between the individual and the nation because the corporation is itself an individual, while at the same time, it transcends individuality because it is immortal, like the imagined nation. And its individuality is not merely a legal fiction (whereby corporations have the rights of citizenship), but an ever-expanding embodiment of experience and feeling. Corporations have experience—or at least, they think they should have them, not merely in the form of institutional memory but increasingly, in the claim (embodied in the proliferation of "non-compete clauses" applied to all workers) that they "own" the experience and not merely the labor time of workers. And within this new cultural imaginary, by the way, it makes perfect sense that Bill Gates would respond to the financial consequences of automation by suggesting that machines pay taxes (rather than holding onto to a more traditionally modern conception of individuals, which might suggest that corporations pay in taxes what they used to pay in wages).

It makes sense then that Trump the person should be the symbolic figure for this emergent political economy as a new

lives—are often nationally branded. Other corporations seem to have no place, while still others—e.g., those that address domestic lives—have distinct national identities in many countries (e.g., Nestlé's—thanks to Megan Wood). In some as yet undefined way, corporations may be reconstituting the relation of the nation as local to the global as placeless, by re-imagining the place not in Cartesian or scalar terms, but as a relational construct at the intersection of spatial vectors. See Saskia Sassen, *Losing Control?* (New York: Columbia University Press, 2015), and Doreen Massey, *Space, Place, and Gender* (Minneapolis: University of Minnesota Press, 1994), and *For Space* (Thousand Oaks, CA.: Sage, 2005).

diagram of governance. On the one hand, his dominant rhetorical appeal is to the use of force and the promise of victory,[36] and he is constantly performing himself as the "strongman." But this is only part of what Trump represents in the popular imagination, for his dominant identification is with the corporate world. Trump is simultaneously the businessman (who seek success at all costs), the CEO or boss (who enforces the rules), and the entrepreneur (who breaks all the rules and invents his own). He is the one who cares about his business precisely because it is his company and his brand, unlike those who control most global corporations and have no personal investment other than greed. Trump can be greedy because he is more than greedy, or rather his greed is articulated affectively to his family and thus, to the nation as identity.[37] And he can be vulgar because his vulgarity is articulated affectively to the state as the force of coercion.[38]

This is an imagined diagram of governance—a form that remediates the relation of the nation and the individual through a re-visioned economy as culture, through the corporate form as culture. It is increasingly common to look to corporations and corporate leaders for moral and political leadership. The corporation resolves the contradiction resulting from the need to reconcile an anti-political cultural nationalism with the inescapable realities of an as yet transitional and unstable global capital. Robocop indeed. Now it is time to panic.

---

36.   Although Bannon, Trump and others seem not to be aware of the culture of the military, defined as it is by honor and duty, or of its commitment to defend the state in the form of the Constitution.

37.   John Clarke in personal conversation has suggested that this new formation might be described in part by re-inflecting Macpherson's concept of possessive individualism into a concern for possessive familialism.

38.   Chris Lundberg suggests that much of Trump's support comes from the assumption that he is willing to take drastic coercive measures to address his supporters' concerns.

8

Conclusions?

If the current conjunctural struggle is a transitional moment, where the old is dying and the new cannot yet be born, I have tried to describe one possible future, one articulation of some of the vectors and forces operating today. Whether it comes to be, whether we allow ourselves to follow this path or not depends on many things. For some, it depends upon articulating a vision of the utopian future, and perhaps of prefiguring that future in the present by constructing local alternatives to the present organizations of sociality and power. Without denying the importance of a positive politics—after all, there are plenty of progressive visions of the future, and they have a long history—I want to leave the matter open because I do not believe that such a politics is likely to be effective, without two other stories: a diagnostic story of where we are, and a strategic story of how we get from here to there (hopefully some place better). Yet they are important because both the right and the left have been fighting a negative politics for too long: the right fighting against liberalism, the left fighting against social and economic injustices. Many of the apparent positive politics of each side are simply the negation of the negation.

I think we begin by recognizing that we have to fight any number of battles across a wide range of issues and fronts, in part because we do not know which if any of these battles will come to define the dominant scenario leading us out of the transition: are we to fight the alt-fascism of a reactionary counter-modernity? the perhaps more likely re-constituted victory of the New Right's expanding hegemony? the possibility of a civil war within the right? or a civil war between the reactionary right and, basically, everyone else who will be seen as liberal, establishment or insufficiently "conservative"? Whatever future unfolds, we must come to terms with the conditions in which we are fighting and we have to keep in mind the various positions, strategies and outcomes against which we may be simultaneously fighting. For example, if it is the construction of chaos in the service of a new political diagram, should we contest it by offering a story about a different organic crisis: a crisis of capitalism without labor, of technology with mediation, of the failure of liberal governmentality, etc.? If it is an authoritarian populism, how do we pose democracy as a viable alternative? If it is, unlike previous New Right constructions, a move away from any hegemonic institutions of politics into more affective realms of rage and hatred on the one hand, and violence and militarization on the other, how do we rebuild faith in a re-imagined configuration of politics, truth and authority? If it is the production of a chaotic ruling bloc in the service of dismantling politics, do we attempt to make the disorganization unbearable, so as to break it apart? At the same time, should we confront what I have suggested is the doubled possibility of a "civil war" (whether politically or violently enacted): a war of the right against their construction of "liberalism" as anti-American, and a war within the right, over the way a century-old history of liberalism is to be undone?

Whatever we might decide will require us to ask, what kind of appeals are we making? How can we reach people "where they are" and move them, however slowly, in the directions we desire? It is not enough to simply offer a clarion call for a "better world," for we must work to win people to that vision, not only as a vision but something that people believe can be accomplished. Does this necessarily mean a politics of compromise and gradualism? Does it mean that we should learn to live with the contradictions, and with the fact that our successes are always limited and incomplete? And how is this even possible given the affective landscape? How do we change that landscape, construct new structures of feeling? Perhaps this is too pessimistic, for the affective landscape is itself complicated and contradictory, and includes both residual and emergent structures of feelings that have yet to be captured by or expelled from the dominant landscape.

Does anyone really think that if Trump supporters (or even anti-Trump conservatives) become disillusioned with Trump, or that if Trump is somehow removed from office, those who have supported him or believe in the new conservatism, or global capitalism, or the New Right, will flock to our side? Perhaps they would look to a left populism, out of anger and frustration, but that is not the best foundation for political change. Perhaps the pendulum would swing yet again. Or perhaps they would follow the logic of alt-fascism: if Trump fails to carry through on his promises, is this not the final proof that democratic state politics cannot succeed? We need to offer something other than the stories we have been telling for decades, which have, in case you have not noticed, largely failed.

While we must address—without panic or hyperactivism—the immediate challenges and devastating damage being done, we also need long-term strategies—both oppositional and visionary, if we are not to continue doing the same things with the same results over and over. We should ask ourselves: why have our tactics over the past fifty years brought only isolated victories, many of which are so fragile that we are already losing some of them and could well lose more in the next years? For those of us who think culture matters, we should ask ourselves how it matters, in what multiple and complex ways is it functioning today, with what appears to be a rather obvious split between a socially liberal mainstream entertainment culture and an increasingly fragmented political culture. Perhaps tactics of mass protest, of visibilization and even disruption, no longer work as they once did. Perhaps these tactics and other forms of symbolic protest do serve an important purpose, to confirm and consolidate the collective and its affective commitment. Perhaps they do allow us to affirm our own moral self-righteousness (and I do not dismiss the need for such self-assurances). But we should also recognize that community and moral witnessing, however important, are not the same as effective political strategy, however we might begin to imagine this. This will require us to question the relation between politics and ethics: the right separates them even as it politicizes ethics, while the left too often conflates them and thus moralizes politics. We should ask ourselves how much of what we are doing, how much of what we take for granted or assume to be benign or even progressive may, in the present conjuncture, have effects or express possibilities that are congruent with some of the forces that we are committed to oppose. This is not to raise accusations of complicity, but to ask how we can understand and meet the demands of the conjuncture. Perhaps the personalization and moralization of politics, for example, no longer serve the ends for which they came into existence, or perhaps we need to question those ends. As Foucault once put it, people know what they are doing but they do not know what they are doing does. That may be as true of the left as of others.

The left—or maybe even more broadly, those of us frightened by what's going on and what it may portend for the future—must be willing to constantly question itself. For example, while the left has, with limited success, touted the benefits of a multicultural society, it has rarely addressed the more difficult question of how such a society is possible, given the constraints of modern common sense. In fact, the defense of multiculturalism has often assumed an additive and rather essentialist understanding, as if multiculturalism were simply the cosmopolitan ability to live with difference, whether by bringing differences into a new unity or by simply denying the need for unity. But multiculturalism, if it is ever to work, has to be imagined differently and more radically. Multiculturalism is the omnipresence of difference, the recognition that difference has been and is always already there in every claim of unity. Every identity is hybrid, always a becoming of another uni-ty-in-difference. It is not that we must fight *for* a multicultural society but for the fact that we have always *been* a multicultural society. But the left has to find ways, even as it questions its own actions and assumptions, and recognizes the complexities and differences, to forge new forms of unity. And it cannot simply celebrate their fragility and temporariness; it must use such unity to construct new stories about the contemporary conjuncture as the means of articulating new, popular agendas for change.

We need to become self-reflective about the relations between our ideas, analyses and practices on the one hand, and the historical and affective contexts in which they exist. If they are to some extent expressions of the structures of feelings out of which they arise, in what ways are they responses, and in what ways might they enhance or constrain our ability to re-articulate them. As I have said, for example, the left's "panic" (even when it is articulated into resistance) may not be an effective strategy to defeat Trump's deployment of panic into resentment. So perhaps we should be fighting against our own affective hyperinflation and anxiety, our obsessive monitoring of everything Trump does, and the expressions of personal hatred that have become increasingly common (even among some of the most intelligent, generous and gentle people I know) and that, all too often, eerily echo the right's absolute hatred of Obama.

This doesn't mean that we should ignore what's going on every day, or the very real threats and consequences of the actions of Trump and his administration, but it does mean that we should temper them with a sense of other temporalities, and other affective possibilities. It means that our political investments cannot be defined only in the immediate present, or even in the short term (of the elections of 2018 and 2020). Again, these are important challenges, but history is made across many timelines.

Long-term strategies take patience and place tactics in the service of something more than a vaguely defined promise or a demand out of time: "We want the world and we want it now" does not get you the world or any significant and lasting piece (peace) of it. This is not compromise but struggle. And long-term strategies demand that one embrace difference in all its forms, including political differences amongst progressives and even amongst those who are not yet willing to embrace progressivism. We must think and plan for all the contingencies, have strategies that address multiple possibilities but are also flexible enough to change course when necessary. We need to be less certain that we already know where we are, where we are going, or where people want to go. And we need to be willing to question our own assumptions, especially the assumption that any moral and rational person would obviously agree with us.

None of this means that symbolic politics is no longer relevant, but we need to appropriate strategies that can challenge or at least re-inflect the claims, allegiances and identifications of those we are opposing and even more importantly, of those we are trying to win to our efforts. As I have said, I believe such struggles must begin where people are, in terms of both affect and common sense. We have to find ways to engage with the languages and logics that people actually use. We have to find ways—both big and small— to change the affective landscape in which people live, recognizing the many different ways in which they live it. Only when we struggle to take this complexity seriously will we be able to engage with and negotiate the affective struggles and contemporary pos- sibilities of political participation and spectatorship. When did we decide to give up the affective power of patriotism? Perhaps we should defend, in popular terms, our "America," and construct the right as un-American, as having abandoned those very principles that "make America great," and which, by the way, the "greatest generation" fought for in World War II. When did we decide to give up the affective power of religion? The figure of Reverend William Barber of North Carolina is one visible exception, but his movement (started as Moral Mondays) does not go far or deep enough. Perhaps we need our own "evangelical" movement, which actually puts forth a vision of religion as a force of peace, love and understanding and speaks out, vociferously and visibly, in the name of Jesus, or King David or Solomon, or Mohammed, etc. against the conservative—and increasingly cruel versions—that seem to dominate public politics. Wouldn't it be amazing if the Pope would excommunicate Catholics who abandoned Jesus' teachings of compassion and charity for all? We must not abandon our visions of hope and our sense of morality, but we must use them more effectively to speak to people who are not yet standing with us.

Does thinking strategically require a generalized attack on capitalism, continuing a long tradition of leftist politics? To be honest, I do not know, but given my argument, it might be more strategic to separate the question of corporations and capitalism, precisely because in the economy's present form, they seem inseparable. This is not to say that the left should not continue to pursue and grow the current interest in socialism, but such feelings may also be an expression of the recognition that the corporate-state relation has failed to produce the "good life" that people want, not only for themselves, but for others and the future. But that failure could easily be re-articulated not to socialism but to alt-fascism. How can we dislodge corporations from their comfortable positions, challenging corporate citizenship and their privileged positions of power? This would require us, above all, to address what seems to be the most perplexing paradox of the current moment: how is it possible that people continue to trust corporations more than government, despite the continuing history of corporate corruption and failure, and the many successes of state intervention and support? How is it that people see corporations rather than the state as providers of hope? But it also means that we have to ask the practical questions: in the face of automation and the massive displacement of jobs, what kinds of responses are both necessary and possible? It is one thing to talk about a basic minimum income, it is another to construct it as a sustainable possibility, and one that still allows for the fact that many people will not be satisfied with this, or that they will think the promise of greater compensation (need it be monetary?) is vital to people's efforts to do more, to accomplish more, to invent more, to create more.

Do we need strategies to re-establish the state as a site of hope? In many ways, the state is still the only form of mediation preventing a variety of forms of social and economic injustice, including alt-fascism. I know that many progressives think the state has failed (agreeing in the end with Bannon), but if we recognize that creating the conditions and perception of state failure has itself been a political strategy, should we not at least consider the question of whether our best alternative is to go along with this? I am not suggesting a return to the state before it came under New Right attack in the 1970s, or before it came under attack in the 1960s from various progressive movements. I am suggesting that we re-imagine the state, that we imagine what course might have been taken if the New Right had not hijacked the left's criticisms of the state. The bureaucratic state was meant to mitigate the discriminatory effects of a state that depended on under-regulated individual decision making, but it has failed and its impersonality and inflexibility have only fed fuel to the New Right's attacks. But the state is an historical invention, and its very form has changed over the past centuries. Rather than abandoning it or restoring it, I am suggesting we try to re-invent it. We must reconfigure the possibilities of sociality and political culture, perhaps harness the new capacities and new forms of sociality already emerging through technology. Maybe that is the new socialism, a new modernity?

Similarly, we might reconsider the party system in general, and the Democratic Party in particular. Both have failed; the former constrains the very possibility of democratic politics, and the latter has long since been seduced by corporate capitalism and wealth.

Yet, if we are to change the possibilities, we will probably have to work through the two-party system in order to move beyond it. That does not mean that we take either the state or the Democratic Party as the parameters of our strategies, but it might suggest that we begin to re-imagine the relations between a democratic movement politics and the state/party. It might mean that we have to recognize that while bottom-up campaigns sponsored by small donations and participatory democracy are morally and symbolically empowering, their effectiveness is always going to be limited. Speaking personally, I find that I am besieged—quite literally—every day—with pleas for donations, and there is a limit not only to my capacity to give, but also to my patience with such appeals. Strategically speaking, we might want to separate, at least for the moment, the rampant and visible greed of contemporary forms of capitalism, from the inevitable inequalities of capitalist economies. We might need to appeal to those capitalists and businesses who are willing to share at least some of our vision of a world that, first, will continue to shelter human life, but more, a world in which social inequalities are challenged and even displaced. To put it bluntly, we might need some of their resources if we are to achieve a world in which they will no longer have so much of the world's wealth. We might convince them that the greatest threat to capitalism at the moment is not anti-capitalism but what the right is doing supposedly in the name of capitalism.[1]

To do any of this, we are going to have to create new forms of cooperation, negotiation and organization, new practices of judgment and authority, with differing degrees and measures of fragility, humility and even temporality, and new models of

---

1. As much as I support a variety of experiments in alternative, local economies, I have yet to see any account that would allow such experiments to replace capitalism in some form. We should remember that capitalism can take on many forms, some seriously worse than others.

conversation and communication.[2] Speaking personally again, I am disheartened by our inabilities to engage in meaningful forms of what I call "convivial agonism," to use language, art and culture to forge unities-in-difference. Even more mundanely, I am discomforted by an endless number of emails, tweets, etc., everyday, many of them redundant, many of them telling me that it is time to panic about one thing or another. I fight against the need to stop them all, to unsubscribe from every progressive listserve. With all our knowledge of social media, is this really the best way to form the bonds of a political community?

In the final analysis, a necessary part, if not the first part, of any answer to the challenges we face is more rigorous thinking—telling better stories, what I might call elitism in the service of democracy, to enable better strategic planning. And given the current context, these stories cannot simply be restoration narratives (always verging on the nostalgic) nor utopian imaginaries (which always sound like they have been on offer for so long). Instead, we will need to recognize the conditions we are living in, the forces operating around us, and the constituencies we must engage. We cannot afford to ignore the actuality of our present, but we also cannot afford to assume that what comes next is pre-ordained either by evolution or catastrophe. The first assumption of politics is that things did not have to be the way they are, and they do not have to continue to be the ways they seem to be heading. Even within the constraints within which we must operate, there are openings, multiple possible configurations, valences and prioritizations, which may lead us away from the nightmare I have described into something somewhat better (even if not yet perfect).

---

2. I have written about such matters in *We All Want to Change the World*, although I would now want to add that one of the great difficulties we face is the possibility of intergenerational conversations, both within the left and across societies more broadly.

Here I must emend a distinction I drew at the very beginning of my reflections on the present moment; I began by distinguishing visionary, diagnostic and strategic stories. Perhaps implicitly, I have written as if the first operated in a different (longer-term) temporality than the latter two. But that is a mistake, for we must overlay this narrative triad on the complexity of temporalities, a complexity that is more than just the continuum from short to long term, a complexity in which the various temporalities are inseparable and mutually determining.

There are then two choices we face immediately. The first involves the question of strategies. What is to be done? Here we must face a stark reality: as the left panics over Trump, it only occasionally notices what will likely emerge in its place (given the affective and political landscapes) without the long and arduous effort of education and articulation: at best another capitalist liberalism, and at worst and more likely, the return of the New Right (Pence as president). I have heard many people say, better the enemy you know than the unpredictability of Trump's administration. Here I simply want to ask whether there is, for the left, a positive side to the chaos. Not only does it mean, in fact, that very little of either Trump's or the New Right's agenda is accomplished, it also means that there is a less structured field of possibilities to be organized. However, this perhaps naïve optimism only works if the left guards against the full range of outcomes, including the most frightening that I have tried to identify here: the rise of a reactionary counter-modernity. To return to the image of a coming civil war, I have often heard progressives talking about a coming civil war. Usually, it goes something like this: if we impeach Trump, then the right will rise up against the liberal establishment (and the various elites). And the story almost always ends with: and remember, they have all the guns. But what if the civil war is coming somewhere else? What if the battle is between the two visions of conservatism? Where can or should progressives choose to stand? Certainly not on one side or the other, and certainly not in the middle. But have we even begun to imagine how to respond to a civil war on the right?

The second choice involves the kind of stories we tell across the various temporal dimensions: do we go on telling the same old stories? Do we tell stories that pretend that it is all new, that we face a new kind of monster unlike anything ever seen before? Or do we tell stories that re-imagine time itself, that re-imagine the very possibility of a future? In the face of the collapse (through its own failures and a variety of attacks), the footholds of European modernity have come undone. Time itself has come undone and it is increasingly difficult to know what it means simply to move forward.[3]

What does it mean to think and do research under such conditions? As Meaghan Morris put it to me, "What are the forms of collective analysis that are possible now, and what new and better forms might emerge, for whom?" But this involves not only seeking empirical methods capable of grasping contemporaneity, nor even constituting modes of collaboration and communication capable of embracing difference and disagreements under the sign of complexity; it is at its heart a question of bringing new political collectivities into existence, new forms and formations of the "we" who can re-invent political imagination without either history or futurity, at least as they have been defined for centuries. Who can agitate for change when the very concept of change has been put under erasure (as Derrida might say)? How do we imagine the present as a field of actualities and possibilities? What if it is imagination itself that is in jeopardy? Imagination dead: imagine. Is this the fascism of our age!

---

3. Some contemporary theorists have offered the concept of transversality to address this question.

Appendix
Cultural Studies and Conjunctural Analysis

Ironically, as much as cultural studies has written about conjunctures, there is no theorized method for such an effort, and even the most cited examples (e.g., Stuart Hall et al., *Policing the Crisis* (London: Macmillan, 1978)) are at best partial and surprisingly not as self-reflective as one might wish. There is no theory that enables one to recognize a conjunctural shift or the emergence of a new organic crisis (rather than another proposed attempt to resolve the crisis). There is no theory that would tell one whether the very concept of an organic crisis is a useful one for a particular context, or if it needs to be radically rethought.[1]

Conjunctural analysis generally equates an empirical description of the political terrain as a war of positions with a sense of the contextual specificity. I propose here to analytically separate these (see Figure 1), to treat the conjuncture as a multidimensional context providing the conditions of possibility of the ground on which a war of positions is waged, and an organic

1.   See John Clarke, "Of Crises and Conjunctures: The Problem of the Present," *Journal of Communication Inquiry* 34(4) (2010): 337–354, and John Clarke and Janet Newman, "'People in this country have had enough of experts': Brexit and the Paradoxes of Populism," *Critical Policy Studies* 11(1) (2017): 101–116. See also my "Wrestling with the angels of cultural studies," in David Morley and Julian Henriques (Eds.). *Stuart Hall: Conversations, Projects and Legacies* (London: Goldsmiths University Press, 2017), pp. 117–126.

crisis takes shape, or where the chaos of uncertainty is itself appropriated as a political strategy. It is here at the intersection of the various historical, political, economic and affective dimensions of lived reality that conjunctural specificity is constituted and defined. In other words, the conjuncture makes possible the war of positions, although the conjunctural conditions are unlikely to correspond directly with the war of positions. It is at the level of

Note: Each level is an expression of/response to—an articulation of relations among—elements of the next (deeper) level. There is no direct/simple correspondence between the elements at different levels.		
Crises are always constructions and therefore sites of struggle at all levels		
War of positions ↓	Sites of (interrelated) struggle	Distributed among multiple, fragmented constituencies/coalitions
	Note: different sites serve different (tactical) functions	
	Sites of (lived) (interrelated) crises, including modes of engagement and consent	Including modes of engagement and consent
Conjunctural analysis as contextualization (what's old and what's new)	*Interacting levels of the conjuncture*	
	Social relations	
	Economic formations and struggles	
	Political formations	The distribution of the field of political positions and struggles
	Political practices	The forms, practices and apparatuses of power and struggle
	Culture as discourse	
	Culture as affective landscape	
Conjunctural specificity					
Diagrammatic analysis: "Ontology" (apparatuses of power) Organic crisis	Dominant				
	Emergent				

Figure 1 A model/method of analysis for the contemporary conjuncture

the conjuncture that the question of an organic crisis has to be raised, and it is at this level that one begins to find expressions of the tectonic struggles over the nature and destiny of a society.

But such struggles cannot finally be understood conjuncturally, for they raise deeper, epochal questions. And this points to yet another—"diagrammatic"—level of analysis, which maps the logics, organizations and apparatuses that constitute the very possibilities of ways of being in the world: Such an historical ontology explores the changing relations and organizations of human and non-human realities, individualities and collectivities, time and space, value and "truth" and the apparatuses of power that construct these relations. These diagrams of the real are not hidden below the surface, the result of some sinister conspiracy or of necessarily repressed forces, available only to a select few, but seeing them demands certain kinds of work to make them visible.

I would hypothesize that some of the "diagrams" that have sustained much of what we take for granted as modernity, each with its own temporality—in some cases since the eighteenth century, in others, since the later part of the nineteenth century and in still others, since the mid-twentieth century—have become increasingly unstable, sometimes directly as a result of intentional struggles and sometimes indirectly as the result of the convergence of forces and struggles without such intentions, and sometimes as the combination or interaction of both.[2] See Figure 2.

---

2. For a discussion of these diagrammatic questions, see my *Cultural Studies in the Future Tense* (Durham, NC: Duke University Press, 2010).

Diagrams/apparatuses in crisis	Subjectivity = consciousness/reason (discipline)	Historicity	Commensuration	Agency = anthropocentrism	Truth: Positivity vs. social construction	Hierarchical/centered space	Sovereignty as nation-state (democracy, consent, consensus)	Identity as social difference (demographics as biopolitics)
Emergent diagrams/apparatuses →	Attention/affect	Immediacy	Unmediated equivalence	Agency as instrumentality	Arbitrary facticity—radical construction	Horizontal—open vs. closed space	Nation as culture/sovereignty as corporate	Identity as culture

Figure 2 Remaking modernity

Bibliography

Electronic resources last accessed July 8, 2017

Alter, Alexandra, "Boom times for the new dystopians." *New York Times.* https://www.nytimes.com/2017/03/30/books/boom-times-for-the-new-dystopians.html?_r=0

Balibar, Etienne, "'Populism' and 'counter-populism' in the Atlantic mirror." http://tinyurl.com/y7498ycm

Bokhart, Allum and Milo Ylannopoulos. "An establishment conservative's guide to the alt-right." www.breitbart.com/tech/2016/03/29/an-establishment-conservatives-guide-to-the-alt-right/

Bond, Becky and Zack Exley, *Rules for Revolutionaries* (White River Junction, VT: Chelsea Green, 2017).

Bray, Mark, *Antifa* (Brooklyn: Melville House, 2017).

Brooks, Arthur C., "Depressed by politics." *New York Times*, March 3, 2017, p. A19.

Brown, Wendy, *States of Injury* (Princeton, NJ: Princeton University Press, 1995).

Cadwalladr, Carole, "Cambridge Analytica affair raises questions vital to our democracy." *Guardian.* https://www.theguardian.com/politics/2017/mar/04/cambridge-analytica-democracy-digital-age

Carnes, Nicholas, and Noam Lupu. "It's time to bust the myth: Most Trump voters were not working class." *Washington Post*, June 5, 2017. http://tinyurl.com/y9dw6fvl

Chua Beng Huat, *Elections as Popular Culture* (London: Routledge, 2007).

—— *Liberalism Disavowed* (Ithaca, NY: Cornell University Press, 2017).

Clarke, John, "Of crises and conjunctures: The problem of the present." *Journal of Communication Inquiry* 34(4) (2010): 337–354.

—— and Janet Newman, "'People in this country have had enough of experts': Brexit and the Paradoxes of Populism." *Critical Policy Studies* 11(1) (2017): 101–116.

Clastres, Pierre, *Society Against the State* (New York: Zone Books, 1989).

Cole, David and Melanie Wachtell Stinnett, *Rules for Resistance* (New York: New Press, 2017).

Cooper, Melinda, *Family Values* (New York: Zone Books, 2017).

Cramer, K.J., *The Politics of Resentment: Rural Consciousness in Wisconsin and the Rise of Scott Walker* (Chicago, IL: University of Chicago Press, 2016).

Davies, Will, "Thoughts on the sociology of Brexit." Political Economy Research Centre, June 24, 2016. www.perc.org.uk/project_posts/thoughts-on-the-sociology-of-brexit/

Davis, Andrew, "Empires with/in/out the State: A conjunctural analysis of corporate sovereignty in the United States." Dissertation, University of North Carolina, 2018.

Derber, Charles, *Welcome to the Revolution* (New York: Routledge, 2017).

DiMaggio, Anthony, *The Rise of the Tea Party* (New York: Monthly Review Press).

Dreher, Richard, *The Benedict Option* (New York: Sentinel, 2017).

Du Bois, W.E.B., *Black Reconstruction in America* (New York: Harcourt Brace, 1935).

Eco, Umberto, "Ur-Fascism." *New York Review of Books*, June 22, 1995. www.nybooks.com/articles/1995/06/22/ur-fascism/

Editors, "Our declaration of independence from the Conservative Movement," July 21, 2016. amgreatness.com/2016/07/21/declaration-independence-conservative-movement/

Editors, "Our policy agenda," May 2017. https://americanaffairsjournal.org/2017/05/our-policy-agenda/

Enzinna, Wes, "This is a war and we intend to win." *Mother Jones*, May–June, 2017. www.motherjones.com/politics/2017/04/anti-racist-antifa-tinley-park-five/

Evola, Julius, *The Revolt Against the Modern World* (Rochester, VT, Inner Traditions, 1995 [1st English edition; original edition 1934]).

Gibson-Graham, J.K., *The End of Capitalism (As We Knew It)* (Minneapolis: University of Minnesota Press, 1996).

Gilroy, Paul, *Against Race* (Cambridge, MA: Harvard University Press, 2002).

Giroux, Henry, *America at War with Itself* (San Francisco, CA: City Lights, 2016).

——— and Brad Evans, *Disposable Futures* (San Francisco, CA: City Lights, 2015).

Goldberg, Michelle, *Kingdom Coming* (New York: W.W. Norton, 2007).

Goldwater, Barry, *With No Apologies* (New York: William Morrow, 1979).

Gramsci, Antonio, *Selections from the Prison Notebooks* (New York: International Publishers, 1971).

Grossberg, Lawrence, *We Gotta Get Out of This Place: Popular Conservatism and Postmodern Culture* (London: Routledge, 1992).

—— *Caught in the Crossfire: Kids, Politics and America's Future* (Boulder, CO: Paradigm, 2005).

—— *Cultural Studies in the Future Tense* (Durham, NC: Duke University Press, 2010).

—— *We All Want to Change the World.* https://www.lwbooks.co.uk/sites/default/files/free-book/we_all_want_to_change_the_world.pdf

—— "Wrestling with the angels of cultural studies," in David Morley and Julian Henriques (eds.). *Stuart Hall: Conversations, Projects and Legacies* (London: Goldsmiths University Press, 2017), pp. 117–126.

Hage, Ghassan, *White Nation: Fantasies of White Supremacy in a Multicultural Society* (London: Routledge, 2000).

—— *Against Paranoid Nationalism* (Annandale, NSW: Pluto Press, 2003).

—— "On stuckedness," in *Alter-Politics* (Melbourne: Melbourne University Press, 2015).

Hall, Stuart, *The Hard Road to Renewal: Thatcherism and the Crisis of the Left* (London: Verso. 1988).

—— "New ethnicities," in Kobena Mercer (ed.). *Black Film, British Cinema, ICA Documents 7* (London: British Film Institute/Institute for Contemporary Arts, 1988), pp. 27–31.

—— "Who needs 'identity'?," in Stuart Hall and Paul du Gay (eds.). *Questions of Cultural Identity* (London: Sage, 1996), pp. 1–17.

—— "The neoliberal revolution." *Cultural Studies* 25 (2011): 705–728.

—— *Cultural Studies 1983* (Durham, NC: Duke University Press, 2017).

—— et al., *Policing the Crisis* (London: Macmillan, 1978).

Hardt, Michael and Antonio Negri, *Empire* (Cambridge, MA: Harvard University Press, 2001).

Harvey, Ofir and Yoram Hazony, "What is Conservatism?" May 2017. https://americanaffairsjournal.org/2017/05/what-is-conservatism/

Hayes, Chris, *Twilight of the Elites* (New York: Broadway Books, 2013).

Hebdige, Dick, "Un-presidented [*sic*]." Lecture presented at the University of California-Santa Barbara's Democracy Day, January 18, 2017.

Hedges, Chris, *American Fascists* (New York: Free Press, 2008).

Hertsgaard, Mark, "Progressives need to build their own media." *The Nation*, March 20, 2017. https://www.thenation.com/article/progressives-need-to-build-their-own-media/

Hibbing, John and Elizabeth Theiss-Morse, *Stealth Democracy* (Cambridge: Cambridge University Press, 2002).

Hochschild, Arlie Russell, *Strangers in Their Own Land* (New York: The New Press, 2016).

Holland, Joshua, "Your guide to the sprawling new anti-Trump resistance movement." *The Nation*, February 6, 2017. https://www.thenation.com/article/your-guide-to-the-sprawling-new-anti-trump-resistance-movement/

Horowitz, Robert B., *America's Right* (Cambridge: Polity, 2013).

Jaffe, Sarah, *Necessary Trouble* (New York: Nation Books, 2016).

Kauffman, L.A., *Direct Action* (London: Verso, 2017).

Kesler, Charles, R. "Trump and the Conservative cause." *Claremont Review of Books*. 16(2) (Spring 2016): 10–16.

Kirk, Russell, *The Conservative Mind* (Washington, D.C.: Regnery, 2001).

Klein, Naomi, *No Is Not Enough* (Chicago, IL: Haymarket, 2017).

Land, Nick, *The Dark Enlightenment*. www.thedarkenlightenment.com/the-dark-enlightenment-by-nick-land/

Leonard, Natasha, "Anti-fascists will fight Trump's fascism in the streets." *The Nation*, January 19, 2017. https://www.thenation.com/article/anti-fascist-activists-are-fighting-the-alt-right-in-the-streets/?print=1

Leonhardt, David and Stuart A. Thompson, "Trump's Lies," *New York Times*, June 23, 2017. https://www.nytimes.com/interactive/2017/06/23/opinion/trumps-lies.html?_r=0

Lichtman, Allan J., *White Protestant Nation* (New York: Atlantic Monthly Press, 2008).

Littler, Jo, *Against Meritocracy* (London: Routledge, 2017).

Lundberg, Christian, "Enjoying God's death: *The Passion of the Christ* and the practices of an evangelical public," *Quarterly Journal of Speech*, 95(4) (November 2009): 387–411.

MacLean, Nancy, *Democracy in Chains* (New York: Viking, 2017).

Marx, Karl, *Capital*. https://www.marxists.org/archive/marx/works/1867-c1/commodity.htm

Massey, Doreen, *Space, Place, and Gender* (Minneapolis: University of Minnesota Press, 1994).

—— *For Space* (Thousand Oaks, CA.: Sage, 2005).

Mellancamp, Patricia, *High Anxiety: Catastrophe, Scandal, Age and Comedy* (Bloomington: Indiana University Press, 1992).

Mirowski, Philip, *Never Let a Good Crisis Go to Waste* (London: Verso, 2013).

Moldbug, Lucius, *Collected Works*. http://moldbuggery.blogspot.com

Morris, Meaghan, *Too Soon Too Late* (Bloomington: Indiana University Press, 1998).

—— "On the future of parochialism: globalization, *Young and Dangerous IV* and Cinema Studies in Tuen Mun," in J. Hill and K. Rockett (eds.). *Film History and National Cinema: Studies in Irish Film 2* (Dublin: Four Courts Press, 2005), pp. 17–36.

Murray, Charles, *Coming Apart* (New York: Crown, 2013).

Neiwert, David, *Alt-America* (London: Verso, 2017).

O'Neill, Cathy, *Weapons of Math Destruction* (New York: Crown, 2016).

Perlstein, Rick, *Before the Storm: Barry Goldwater and the Unmaking of the American Consensus* (New York: Hill and Wang, 2001).

Phillips-Fein, Kim, *Invisible Hands* (New York: Norton, 2009).

Plan C, "We are all very anxious." http://tinyurl.com/y9ywtzgm

Publius Decius Mus, "The Flight 93 election," September 5, 2016. www.claremont.org/crb/basicpage/the-flight-93-election/

Robin, Corey, *The Reactionary Mind* (Oxford: Oxford University Press, 2013).

Ross, Alexander Reid, *Against the Fascist Creep* (Chico, CA.: AK Press, 2017).

Rothman, J., "The lives of poor white people." *The New Yorker*. September 12, 2016. www.newyorker.com/culture/cultural-comment/the-lives-of-poor-white-people

Sassen, Saskia, *Losing Control?* (New York: Columbia University Press, 2015).

Schudson, Michael, *Origins of the History of Objectivity in the Professions: Studies in the History of American Journalism and American Law 1830–1940* (New York: Garland, 1990).

Scott, David, *Conscripts of Modernity* (Durham, NC: Duke University Press, 2004).

Sharma, Sarah, *In the Meantime* (Durham, NC: Duke University Press, 2014).

Smucker, Jonathan, *Hegemony How-to* (Chico, CA.: AK Press, 2017).

Smythe, Dallas, "Communications: Blindspot of Western Marxism." *Canadian Journal of Political and Social Theory*, 1(3) (Fall 1977): 1–28.

Solnit, Rebecca, *Hope in the Dark* (New York: Disruption Books, 2017).

Strauss, William and Neil Howe, *The Fourth Turning: An American Prophecy* (New York: Broadway Books, 1997).

Suskind, Ron, "Faith, certainty and the presidency of George W. Bush." *New York Times Magazine*, October 17, 2004. www.nytimes.com/2004/10/17/magazine/faith-certainty-and-the-presidency-of-george-w-bush.html?_r=0

Taibbi, Matt, *Insane Clown President* (New York: Spiegel & Grau, 2017).

Toscano, Alberto, *Fanaticism* (London: Verso, 2010).

Trilateral Commission, *The Crisis of Democracy* (1975). http://trilateral.org/download/doc/crisis_of_democracy.pdf

Vance, J.D., *Hillbilly Elegy* (New York: Harper Collins, 2016).

Waltman, Mike, *Hate on the Right* (New York: Peter Lang, 2014).

Whippman, Ruth, *America the Anxious* (New York: St. Martin's, 2016).

Williams, Raymond, *The Long Revolution* (London: Chatto and Windus, 1961).

—— *The Country and the City* (New York: Oxford University Press, 1973).

—— *Marxism and Literature* (Oxford: Oxford University Press, 1978).

Wood, Megan and Ryan Brownlow, "Not about white workers," *Lateral*, forthcoming.

Žižek, Slavoj, *The Sublime Object of Ideology* (London: Verso, 1989).

Thanks

I begin by thanking John Clarke, Meaghan Morris, John Pickles and Christian Lundberg. Large parts of this book are the fruition of years of wonderful conversations with them. Also Megan Wood, Carey Hardin, Allison Schlobohm, Andrew Davis, Bryan Behrenshausen, Jennifer Daryl Slack, Ted Striphas, Dick Hebdige, Ken Wissoker, Henry Giroux and Paul Gilroy have helped me enormously. In addition to being the author of this book, I have also been a collaborator, collector, curator and interlocutor. I started this project hoping to offer a truly collective and collaborative work, using the institutional conventions of academic work—classes, workshops, networks—but I failed. Still, even a failed effort can accomplish important things. So I want to thank the students in my cultural studies seminar (Ryan Brownlaw, Xuenan Cao, Nicole Castro, Rocio Corral Garcia, Izaak Earnhardt, Marie Ensenyi, Jack Ewing, David Farrow, Blake Faulkner, Sherah Faulkner, Jing Jiang, Alexander Marsden, Smita Misra, Emily Moran, Logan Parke, Lucas Power, Manuel Sanchez Cabrera, Joshua Scalzetti, Allison Schlobohm, Sarah Tomlinson, Amaia Valparis, Megan Wood), and my colleagues from the Conjunctures Workshop (Anne Balsamo, Ron Greene, Gil Rodman, Greg Seigworth, Jennifer Daryl Slack, Ted Striphas, Patty Sotirin and Greg Wise). I also want to admit that I have no doubt taken ideas and insights from the literally hundreds of essays and articles I have read over the past months, even if they remain traces without an inventory. Finally, I want to thank David Castle and the "team" at Pluto Press for all their efforts and support.